THE DIY
STYLE
Finder

KariAnne Wood

HARVEST HOUSE PUBLISHERS
EUGENE, OREGON

Unless otherwise indicated, Scripture quotations are from the Holy Bible, New International Version®, NIV®. Copyright © 1973, 1978, 1984, 2011 by Biblica, Inc.® Used by permission. All rights reserved worldwide.

Cover by Nicole Dougherty

Interior design by Faceout Studio

Photos on pages 12, 19, 21, 23, 25, 27, 48, 49, 56 (object photos); 57, 79 (Farmhouse mantle); 80, 81, 88, 89, 112, 113, 120, 121, 143 (Coastal hutch); 144, 145, 151, 170, 171, 194, 195, 202, 203, 216, 217, 220, 221, 223 by KariAnne Wood.

Photos of Yvonne (10, 88), Bre (10 , 120), Laura (11 , 202), and Carmel (11 , 170) provided by each homeowner respectively. Used by permission. All other photography by Jay Eads

Published in association with William K. Jensen Literary Agency, 119 Bampton Court, Eugene, Oregon 97404

The DIY Style Finder

Copyright © 2019 by KariAnne Wood

Published by Harvest House Publishers

Eugene, Oregon 97408

www.harvesthousepublishers.com

ISBN 978-0-7369-7228-4 (Hardcover)

ISBN 978-0-7369-7229-1 (eBook)

Library of Congress Cataloging-in-Publication Data

Names: Wood, KariAnne, author.

Title: The DIY style finder / KariAnne Wood.

Description: Eugene, Oregon : Harvest House Publishers, [2019]

Identifiers: LCCN 2018022894 (print) | LCCN 2018023070 (ebook) | ISBN 9780736972291 (ebook) | ISBN 9780736972284 (hardcover)

Subjects: LCSH: Interior decoration--Amateurs' manuals.

Classification: LCC NK2115 (ebook) | LCC NK2115 .W8297 2019 (print) | DDC 747--dc23

LC record available at https://lccn.loc.gov/2018022894

Printed in China

18 19 20 21 22 23 24 25 26 27 /IM-FO / 10 9 8 7 6 5 4 3 2 1

To Denny

I think a little piece of me fell in love with you the first time we ever met.

Before you became my best friend

Before you became my one and only.

Before I ever really knew the wonder that is you.

Remember the first apartment with the plastic furniture?

Remember our journey across America in a car without air-conditioning?

Remember every inside joke we ever told?

Remember how we always said it was *us* against the world?

I do.

And I would live this life over again and again and again.

If I could live it with you.

Contents

Introduction

I can't decide if I should introduce myself first or start right in on the cartwheels now that you're here.

I can't help it.

I'm all about an over-the-top gymnastic celebration.

My mother always told me that when you meet someone truly amazing (*just like you*) and you're thrilled and excited and you want to say hello, but you're a little unsure on how to take the first step, you take a breath. Press pause. And go all Julie Andrews and start at the beginning.

I'm KariAnne.

I wear yoga pants and messy buns and purple nail polish and currently own almost every shade of red lipstick on the planet. I watch Hallmark movie marathons, and I have hands that wave when I talk and oddly long toes, and I spend my days trying to find homes for abandoned furniture. I've been decorating since my first Barbie house, and I love a DIY, and for seven years I've written a blog called *Thistlewood Farms*.

I remember the first day I started the blog.

I had big plans. It was going to be detailed and full of decorator terminology and important, meaningful words of wisdom and lengthy discussions about what to do and what not to do when decorating your home. At the time, I had no idea how to take pictures. I used disposable cameras that were yellow. *You know.* The ones you took to Walgreens and then threw away after you used them.

I hired a photographer, and he came to the house and took the most incredible pictures of my Christmas decorations. I still remember when he sent the photographs to me. I sat at the computer staring in wonder. I was in awe. I was so full of joy. At the risk of stating the obvious, my Christmas decorating was on fleek. I couldn't wait to show the world.

Oh, the blog I was going to write!

I sat down at the computer with words swirling around in my head about neutrals and Christmas trees and why gray was so 2011. I added the first picture to the post and smiled. It was amazing. Didn't my chairs match my ottoman and pick up the tiny flecks of silver in my stockings hung by the fireplace perfectly? And the tree? Had the world ever seen such a tree? It was nine feet tall and covered with glittery ornaments and snowflakes and twinkling stars and pinecones and...*and...and...*

...WHAT WAS THAT?

There, at the bottom of the photograph, were the giant metal feet of the tree. It was awful. It was terrible. And to make matters worse, the wide-angle lens only amplified them in all their metalness and made them appear as if they were taking over the room. *How had that happened?* How had I forgotten the first rule of Christmas decorating? What was I thinking?

My room was decorated without a tree skirt.

The fancy decorating blog never happened. The pearls of wisdom never showed up. On that long ago first day of the blog, I never wrote the post I intended to.

Instead?

I wrote about celebrating imperfection and living with what you have and learning from mistakes and skirtless trees and the people who love them. Every day, every week, every month I shared things that inspired me and how to decorate with what you have and letting your house reflect you. And along the way, something incredible happened. I discovered a world of people who were just like me.

People who loved their homes.

People who wanted to decorate without all the fancy words and fancy explanations and rules and guidelines.

People who wanted to decorate with their heart.

This book is an extension of that message. It's all about finding a design style and building a room by room design framework and learning what works in your home. The book is filled with inspiration and creative ideas and layering in pattern and color and texture to fit different styles.

And now?

Before we get started, I wanted to point out the obvious and something you're probably already thinking at this point because we both know how

brilliant you are—there are enough decorating styles in the world to fill an entire set of encyclopedias from A to Z. I couldn't cover them all within the pages of this book, so I did the next best thing. To make it easier, I chose five major categories of design styles to work with. Within these pages, we'll look at traditional, farmhouse, transitional, contemporary, and coastal.

But here's the thing.

Before we start. Before we turn the next page. Before we take the quiz and determine what our design style is. Before we check one single box.

I want to give you permission…

…to be YOU.

You probably identify with one particular style more than others; however, there may be elements of different design styles outlined in the book that speak to your heart. If your style is traditional, but you love driftwood? Use it. If your style is farmhouse, but a colorful, eclectic accessory calls your name? Answer. If your style is coastal, but you decide you can't live without a set of wingback chairs? Bring them home and introduce them to your conch shells.

Let your style inspire you instead of define you.

Because in all this world, there is only one you.

Now grab your paper and your pen and your imagination. This is the start of an exciting design journey. Inspiration and style ideas and creative design solutions are just pages away. Embrace your style and your heart and get ready to create a home that's amazing.

Exactly like you.

Meet Our Homeowners

When I decided I wanted to write a book about decorating and the styles that love it, I knew I needed a little help—a little extra assistance. So I went to the top—to experts who inspire me—and asked for advice. I've included four of the most creative, innovative, and incredible individuals I know, along with a tour of my family's beach home. Each of our homes is decorated with heart. Each of our styles is different. Each of our homes is unique. Come along with me as we explore each of the five homes and meet the friends who took a decorating style and made it their own.

Yvonne

TRADITIONAL

Yvonne journals her adventures on the popular home décor blog, *StoneGable*. She is an empty nester and lives with her husband, Bobby, in the middle of picturesque Amish Country in Pennsylvania. Yvonne is a lifelong learner on a quest for new things to learn and do, and she shares her creative ideas with her readers along with unique DIY projects and simple recipes. She lives by grace and strives to be positive and purposeful—living large and loving everyone who crosses her path. Her front door is always open to friends old and new.

Favorites

COLOR: Cornflower blue
ROOM: Kitchen
DESSERT: Chocolate chip cookies
MOVIE: *Sense and Sensibility*

Bre

FARMHOUSE

Bre is the author and creative voice behind the blog *Rooms for Rent*, with its signature simple approach to design. This wife and mom decorates with her heart and believes that no matter if you are renting or own your home, if you're an empty nester, or if you're living in your first apartment, everyone can "love the space they live in." Growing up in New England has shaped Bre's love for historic architecture, country settings, and coastal homes—all things that inspire her when she's creating spaces that are relaxed and comfortable with classic appeal.

Favorites

COLOR: White
ROOM: Living room
DESSERT: A warm chocolate chip cookie
MOVIE: *The Notebook*

TRANSITIONAL

Laura writes the home décor blog *Finding Home Farms* to share creative ideas, home projects, and inspirational "befores" and "afters." Laura and her husband, Dana, a fourth-generation sugar maker, live in the Hudson Valley. Together, the Putnams have built a growing maple sugar business on the foundation of family and home. *Finding Home Farms* is all about celebrating farm to table, the heart of family, and warm and welcoming spaces.

Favorites

COLOR: Green
ROOM: Screened-in porch
DESSERT: Apple cider doughnuts
MOVIE: *It's a Wonderful Life*

CONTEMPORARY

Carmel is in the process of remodeling her current home and chronicles her adventures on the pages of her blog, *Our Fifth House*. She believes in creating happy spaces that are fun and not complicated. She designs her life and her projects according to her motto: "A home should reflect the personality of the people who live under its roof." Carmel's work has been featured in *Family Circle*, *All You*, and *Cottages and Bungalows*. Carmel lives with her family in historic South Carolina.

Favorites

COLOR: Red
ROOM: Home office
DESSERT: Anything with chocolate
MOVIE: *Father of the Bride*

COASTAL

KariAnne writes the decorating and lifestyle blog *Thistlewood Farms* from her project-filled 1908 home in Dallas, Texas. She recently followed God's call and jumped back "home" with her family from the middle of the country to the busy Dallas Metroplex, where she lives with her husband and four children. The blog was awarded Country Living Decorating Blog of the Year as well as named one of the Top 10 Decorating Blogs by *Better Homes and Gardens*. KariAnne's work has been featured in *Better Homes and Gardens Christmas Ideas*, *Country Living*, *Flea Market Décor*, and many others.

Favorites

COLOR: Gray with a hint of khaki
ROOM: Laundry room
DESSERT: Chocolate chip cookies
MOVIE: *Steel Magnolias*

Style Quiz

What is it about design that makes you smile? What makes your décor heart beat faster? What type of accessories and lamps and rugs and paint colors and wall art and furniture do you want to bring home to meet your house?

Truth?

It's the one question we all ask ourselves. The one question inquiring design minds want to know. The question we ponder standing in the middle of the pillow aisle in our favorite home décor store.

What is my style?

You ask questions. We have answers. Here's a little quiz to help you figure out what your style looks like. Quizzes like this can be a little challenging because sometimes more than one answer fits or none of the answers seem like a fit. That's okay. If none of the answers (or too many of the answers) are a fit, simply select one answer that is the closest to how you see your style.

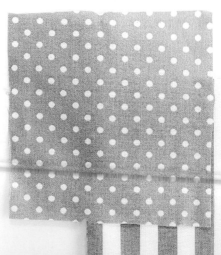

1 What do you value in your home?

A. Consistency, familiarity, and order

B. Warmth, hospitality, and tradition

C. Uniqueness, personality, and history

D. Style, energy, and openness

E. Comfort, the outdoors, and relaxation

2 What colors are you drawn to?

A. Deep, rich tones—navy, burgundy, emerald green

B. Neutrals—white, gray, beige, tan

C. Eclectic—purple, lavender, gold, fuchsia, aqua

D. Bold, bright, energetic—red, pink, orange, blue

E. Natural, earthy tones—light greens, light blues, white, beige

3 What are some of your favorite patterns?

A. Stripes, damask, toile

B. Gingham, floral, ticking

C. Embroidered fabric, vintage patterns, heirloom prints

D. Graphic prints, stripes, oversized geometric, animal print

E. Stripes, whimsical prints, ombré patterns

4 How do you accessorize?

A. Antique china, brass candlesticks, collectibles

B. DIY frames, reclaimed baskets, mismatched dishes

C. Family photos, heirloom pieces, repurposed architectural elements

D. Unique statement pieces, pops of color, bold artwork

E. Natural wood pieces, baskets, driftwood

Damask

An ornately patterned fabric usually printed on linen or cotton. The pattern can be seen on both sides and is typically a larger-scale pattern.

Toile

Fabric featuring bucolic scenes printed on white or off-white fabric.

Ticking

Originally used to cover mattresses and pillows, this utilitarian fabric features a series of tiny vertical stripes.

Ombre

This color technique highlights the blending of one shade of a color into another, starting with the darkest shade and continuing the technique to the lightest shade.

5 Favorite textures and materials?

A. Porcelain, polished wood, plush rugs or textiles

B. Galvanized metal, linen, chippy wood, baskets, burlap

C. Mix of reclaimed wood, unusual finishes, painted patinas, upholstered pieces

D. Glass, mirrored pieces, fur, acrylic, mixed-metal finishes

E. White wood paneling, natural fibers, sea glass, stones, reclaimed wood

6 What shapes or lines are you drawn to?

A. Curved lines, intricate details, symmetry, classic detailing

B. Straight lines, simple shapes, imperfect details

C. Architectural pieces, intricate patterns

D. Clean lines, sleek shapes, precise details

E. Organic lines, shapes, nature-inspired details

7 My home slogan would be...

A. I never met a blue-and-white plate I didn't like.

B. Pass the sweet tea.

C. You won't believe what I made with my grandmother's needlepoint.

D. Isn't zebra print a neutral?

E. Open the windows and let the sunshine in.

8 I would never, ever decorate with...

A. Driftwood and sea glass

B. Leopard print or faux black fur

C. A prescribed room model

D. Distressed, chippy items

E. Heavy, plush fabrics or acrylic furniture

Patina

The surface texture and layers of paint and/or oxidized finish on a piece of metal or wood. Patina is typically created over time with age but can be mimicked with faux finishes.

9 **I'm inspired by architecture and design from...**

A. The Victorian era

B. Early Americana

C. My family home

D. NYC

E. Cape Cod

10 **You collect...**

A. China

B. Mason jars

C. Door knobs

D. Colorful art

E. Sand dollars

11 **The perfect rug for my home would be...**

A. Oriental

B. Jute

C. Vintage

D. Geometric

E. Sea grass

12 **You're hosting a dinner. What's on the table?**

A. Mercury glass candlesticks, wedding china, linen napkins with a classic ring

B. Fresh greenery, milk jug vases, fresh produce, white dishes

C. Two patterns of Grandma's china, a vintage toolbox filled with flowers, cutting board chargers

D. Bold, patterned dishes; colorful, narrow-stemmed vases; metallic chargers

E. Blue-and-white dishes, driftwood, blue glass vases

Americana
A décor style that celebrates American heritage and features flags, pennants, and distressed red, white, and blue accessories.

Jute
Natural fiber woven into twine made from plants and then woven into rugs, textiles, and baskets.

Mercury glass
This type of glass is manufactured using a process that creates layers of speckles and streaks on the surface of the glass.

Tufted

An upholstery treatment for furniture using buttons. String is attached to the button and pulled tightly, dividing the fabric into sections.

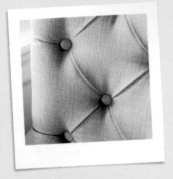

Rattan

Furniture made from strips of wood from different varieties of palm.

Macramé

A woven textile comprised of a series of knots.

Pop art

This type of art emerged in the 1950s, featuring bold colors and advertising imagery.

13 **What's your go-to chair?**

A. Tufted wingback

B. Rattan armchair

C. Upholstered chair with mismatched ottoman

D. Leather chair with metal accents

E. Adirondack chair

14 **What kind of artwork are you drawn to?**

A. Botanicals

B. Vintage signs

C. Macramé

D. Bold abstracts

E. Landscapes

 What one item would you *have* to buy at a yard sale?

A. Antique hutch

B. Antique milk can

C. Eclectic lamp in your favorite color

D. Pop art

E. Wicker dining set

Scoring

Go back through your answers and tally how many **A**s, **B**s, **C**s, **D**s, and **E**s you scored.

> If you scored mostly **A**s, turn to page 18-19 to see your style.
>
> If you scored mostly **B**s, turn to page 20-21 to see your style.
>
> If you scored mostly **C**s, turn to page 22-23 to see your style.
>
> If you scored mostly **D**s, turn to page 24-25 to see your style.
>
> If you scored mostly **E**s, turn to page 26-27 to see your style.

It's important to understand that this quiz is here to provide a framework for your style journey. When you answered the questions, you may have discovered one style that truly stood out to you.

Congratulations. *You have a clearly defined sense of what your style is.*

But what if you didn't discover that one style? What if the quiz was challenging for you? What if you wanted to check one or two or *all of the boxes* on some of the questions?

Congratulations. *You have a style that's distinctly your own.*

The styles in this book are just that—descriptions of how different individuals decorate their homes. They are meant to be a resource. A guide. *A road map.* An inspiration. *The DIY Style Finder* was created to define certain styles so you can select elements that work together to create a look that's transitional or coastal or contemporary or farmhouse or traditional or some combination thereof that works for YOU.

Come join me on the journey. Step into the pages of this book. Together we'll decorate and plan and design and find a style that is unique and creative and special and original and distinctive and one-of-a-kind and extraordinary.

Just. Like. You.

TOTAL DECORATING ASIDE: If you are still feeling a little lost at this point, why not take a second look at transitional? It's a little more eclectic than the other styles. If you like to combine different elements of different design styles, transitional may be the style for you.

Traditional Style Defined

If you scored mostly *As*, congratulations. Your style is traditional! Traditional style is a lot like its name—full of tradition. It's all about antiques that may or may not have come over on the Mayflower and thick, plush rugs and blue-and-white china and crisp white moldings and beautiful artwork that looks as if it was handed down from your great-great-great-grandmother. Traditional style feels as though the home has always been here. It's classic. It's timeless. It will still be holding up its head and its style for years to come. Walking through the halls of a home decorated with traditional style, you might see a beautiful hand-carved mantel surrounded by antique chairs reupholstered in a tiny check print and fluffed with beautiful damask pillows. Or the patina of a timeworn hutch filled with blue-and-white china next to boxwood topiaries.

It's the celebrate forever style. It's the put-out-your-grandmother's-china-for-dinner style. It's the white linen and buffalo check pillows and sparkling crystal chandelier and timeless stand-the-test-of-time antique rug kind of style.

This style is for everyone who has ever talked to an antique or styled a bookcase with blue-and-white porcelain dogs or flipped the switch on a thousand twinkles over their dining table. If you love décor that doesn't change its mind every year; if you think antiques should be collected, not painted; if you love classic fabrics and texture and colors, this is the style for you. Traditional style is all about choosing classic and timeless pieces to build on and creating a room that is here to stay.

Farmhouse Style Defined

If you scored mostly *B*s, congratulations. Your style is farmhouse! If you've met me for more than five minutes, you know that farmhouse style is my heart. I can't help it. I first found my decorating voice at Thistlewood. Farmhouse style is all about celebrating the chippy, the worn, the distressed, and every barn door that has ever gone before. Homes decorated in farmhouse style feel warm and welcoming, with vintage and texture layered in. If you were to walk through a house decorated in farmhouse style, you might see a chicken coop used as a coffee table and topped with baskets filled with books and magazines. Or a giant, galvanized windmill hanging over a chippy wood mantel styled with hand-turned candlesticks and barn wood signs.

It's the turn trash into treasure style. It's the flip the script on windows and doors and architectural pieces you find by the side of the road kind of style. It's the galvanized metal and willow baskets and reclaimed wood and walls of white yard sale plates kind of style.

Farmhouse style is for everyone who has ever seen chicken coops or winding country roads or hay bales or the faded red wood on a barn and fallen in love. If you love vintage, if you have ever bought a quilt at a yard sale just to rescue it for future projects, if you think all furniture looks better with a little character and some milk paint, then this is the style for you. Farmhouse is all about celebrating friends and family and all the grain sacks that have ever lived and creating spaces that feel like home.

Transitional Style Defined

If you scored mostly Cs, congratulations. Your style is transitional! Transitional style is all about celebrating the unique. The eclectic. The innovative. The one of a kind. Homes decorated with transitional style elements often combine pieces from different décor styles in a creative and unconventional way. Walking through the rooms of a transitional style home, you might see a wall of family heirlooms hung over a farmhouse hutch with brilliant brass hardware. Or a vintage kilim rug tucked under an antique sideboard topped with a collection of milk glass vases. Or a driftwood wreath hung on a set of antique windows next to a colorfully painted thrift store find.

It's the make it your own style. It's the bring it home if you love it style. It's the find a place for something that makes you smile style.

Transitional style is for the fearless, for the bold, for the individual carving his or her own decorating path. If you aren't really a rule follower, if you march to the beat of your own decorating drum, if you like your farmhouse pillow on a bright orange chair, then this is the style for you. Transitional is all about taking the things that you love—whatever the style, whatever the look—and creating a home that's uniquely you.

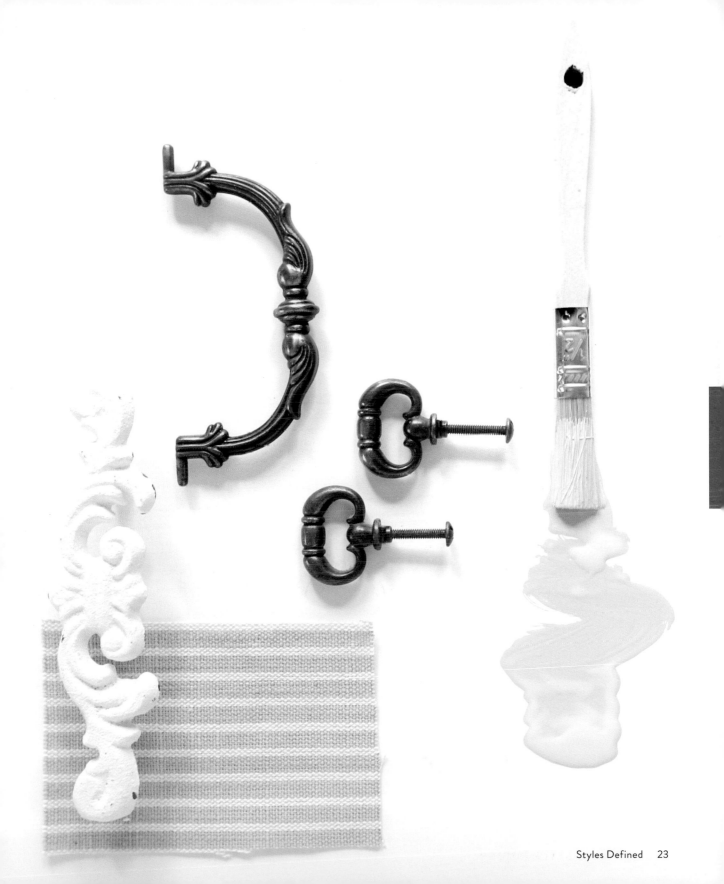

Contemporary Style Defined

If you scored mostly *D*s, congratulations. Your style is contemporary! Contemporary style brings the fun and the joy to design. It's all about sparkling glass tabletops and chairs you can see through and clever graphic designs and leopard print chair covers. It's exciting. It's irreverent. It's vibrant. If you visit a home decorated with contemporary style, you might see classic architecture mixed with bright colors and graphic textiles and brass fixtures. Or you may see rooms with brilliantly colored upholstered pieces next to mirrored glass end tables topped with clean-lined frames filled with brightly patterned artwork.

It's a fresh approach to design. It's all about the here and the now and the current. It's bright red, fuzzy pillows fluffed onto turquoise chairs placed atop a striped black-and-white rug style. It's a pale pink space popped with oversized graphic prints next to an arrangement of succulents in a brilliant blue planter type of style.

Contemporary is for all the trendsetters who decorate with abandon and fill their homes with laughter. If you love bright colors, if you are all about a navy and orange and hot pink patterned rug, if you think design should make your heart laugh out loud, then contemporary is the style for you.

Coastal Style Defined

If you scored mostly *E*s, congratulations. Your style is coastal! I was raised on coastal style. Truly. I spent every summer on the shores of Cape Cod Bay bringing home shells and driftwood and sea glass and stones to decorate my room. But coastal style is so much more than that. It's a feeling of simplicity mixed with sea breezes and sunshine. It's fresh. It's welcoming. It's the joy of a long summer day spent with the wind at your back and the sun on your face. If you enter a home decorated with coastal style, you might see fresh textiles, such as stripes and polka dots juxtaposed with natural fibers. Or see white linen sheets tucked into a painted wood bed next to an inlaid dresser that is topped with a string of seashells.

It's celebrate the everyday style. It's collect colorful sea glass in a jar and add pillows to Adirondack chairs and cut fresh hydrangea style. It's place a driftwood bowl on the coffee table and make a flag out of sand dollars and starfish kind of style.

Coastal is for everyone who has ever written love letters in the sand or stood on a beach and watched the waves crash on the shore or hung sheets out to dry in the summer sun. If you love natural elements, if you think shells should double as decorations, if you believe watermelon should be a main course, and if you love sunbeams dancing across wide pine planks—then coastal is the style for you.

The Entryway

1

Where Home Greets You at the Front Door

When I grew up and got highlights and Lee Press-On Nails and stirrup pants and went away to college to take on the world, every couple of months or so I'd go back to my hometown. Mostly to visit or do laundry or talk my parents into a tank of gas. Whichever came first. I'd pull into the driveway and leap out of the car and throw open the door and step into the entryway.

And home would come rushing in.

It was all there. The smells. The sights. The sounds. The creak of the vintage wood floors. The shine of the windows. The sunlight dancing across the room.

Wouldn't it be amazing if life were a lot like entryways?

Always a new beginning. Always a fresh start. Always walking in with your best foot forward. Always welcoming. Always home.

Your entryway is the place where first impressions start. Sometimes good. Sometimes maybe not so much. We once had an Easter egg hunt at our house with real Easter eggs. *You know.* The kind you hard-boil and dip in dye and sprinkle with glitter. We hid eggs and candy all over the house, and our children went on a hunt and filled up their Easter baskets with treasures.

Except.

Except they left one Easter egg behind. No one missed it. No one knew. Until a month later when the front entry started to smell. You barely noticed it at first. I wrinkled my nose and brushed it off and went on. But the smell got worse. And worse. Until one day it was so bad my guests didn't even want to step inside the front door until they put a hazmat suit on. *Yikes.*

The moral of this dairy tale? Never underestimate the power of really good air freshener.

In addition to double-checking your entryway for eggs, here are a few tips and ideas to create a warm and welcoming space that reflects your personality and your decorating style.

Introduce Your Style

If a home's style is written on the pages of its rooms, then the entryway is the introduction. Allow guests to glimpse your personal decorating style from the first step through the front door. If coastal is your style, add a driftwood mirror. If you like traditional? Layer in an antique rug. It doesn't have to be an overwhelming statement piece—just a hint of the decorating personality that's just around the corner.

Light It Up

Create a welcoming entry with a little light. Place a small bookshelf or hutch in the entryway and add a lamp. Spotlight a piece of art on the wall. Add sconces to either side of the front door to warm up the entrance. In addition, adding a dimmer to your lighting helps change the mood depending on the time of day.

Look Down

Placing a rug in the entryway immediately warms up the room. Area rugs provide a cushion and introduce pattern and color into the small space.

tip The entryway is a high-traffic area. You'll want to make sure to select a durable, stain-resistant rug for the floor. The one I chose works perfectly. It's the color of dirt.

Provide a Surface for Stuff

There's nothing like an entry to attract all kinds of stuff. I walk in with mail, keys, a purse, and the occasional umbrella. Think through all that stuff. Give it a place to land. A small console or table is the perfect piece for an entryway, especially if it has drawers. You might also want to add baskets to the tabletop to keep everything organized.

tip Adding a charging station to your entryway is a great way to keep your devices ready for the next trip.

Extra Seating

If your space allows, add a small chair with a little personality to the entryway. This is a great way to introduce a little style. For example, if your style is contemporary, choose a bright, geometric pattern to add a pop of color to the space. If transitional is more your look, add a pillow to the chair with one of your favorite quotes.

Faux Your Entryway

It's important to remember that not every house has an entryway. No worries. If you don't have an extra room by the front door, just faux it. Create the look of an entry with furniture and accessories. Add a hutch or bookcase by the front door with extra lighting and small bins for keys. Place a smaller rug just inside the door to define your entryway space. In addition, add an umbrella stand or oversized baskets by the entry for storage.

Traditional Style

If you think traditional style is where it's at, this is the entryway for you. If antique pieces and damask fabric and patterned rugs and blue-and-white china and clocks that chime make your heart sing, here are a few traditional design elements to show off your personality in your entryway.

WALL ART

Framed art is the perfect way to add a little traditional style to your walls. Group framed pieces together in linear rows of three or four prints. If original artwork is a little too pricy for your budget, frame florals or drawings from the pages of a vintage book instead. Another option would be a gold leaf mirror to add a little shine to your space. Add carved wood shelves on either side of the mirror and top with a blue-and-white porcelain piece.

STORAGE

One fun way to create storage for a traditional entryway is to repurpose an antique piece. Rich, dark wood and timeworn patinas make any antique the perfect fit. Use an antique dresser and all its drawers for storage. Place an antique bookcase against the wall, and place baskets on each of the shelves to tuck scarves and purses out of sight. Tie labels to the baskets or paint a monogram to add a unique traditional element that fits your style.

RUGS

Rich, vibrant colors work well when selecting a rug for the entryway. Traditional rug patterns and thick, rich pile help create the feeling of timelessness. Another option might be a vintage kilim rug. The dark navy blue and tomato reds of many kilim rugs anchor the entryway and create a warm and welcoming feel in the room. Shop for vintage rugs at estate sales and online marketplaces to find one that is right for your space.

SEATING

If your entryway is large enough, a wingback chair makes the perfect accent piece. If space is at a premium, choose a smaller, spindle-back chair or other accent wood chair with a beautiful antique patina. Warm up the wood with vibrant textiles, and toss a throw over the back of the chair to bring in another element of traditional style.

TEXTILES

Traditional style is all about pattern. Choose fabrics with an overall pattern, such as damask or paisley or houndstooth. Pair an overall pattern like this with a smaller pattern, such as a stripe or check. These textiles come in a variety of colors, from brilliant hues of purple and red and navy to a softer palette of creams and grays and yellow. Select the color that fits your style best, and let your personality shine.

Farmhouse Style

If farmhouse style is your thing, this is the entryway for you. If chippy tables and galvanized metal and chicken crates turned into coffee tables make your heart sing, here are a few design elements to show off your personality in your entryway.

WALL ART

If you are farmhouse, then you are probably a collector of all things vintage. Sometimes you buy it and have no idea what to do with it. You just love it. A gallery wall is your solution. In your entryway, fill up a blank wall with your collection. Mix in family photos and architectural salvage and framed vintage hand towels and the violin you inherited from your uncle. If it makes your heart smile, frame it and hang it up.

STORAGE

Farmhouse is all about galvanized metal and vintage syrup buckets and apple crates and rag baskets. Add a little character to your space and use containers like these to keep your front entry organized. If space is tight in the entryway, any of these vintage finds can also be repurposed and hung on the wall for vertical storage.

RUGS

Add farmhouse style to your entry with a natural fiber rug. Sea grass, jute, and sisal are all durable rugs, perfect for the high traffic of an entryway. Vintage rag rugs and braided rugs add a little color to a space and immediately warm up an entryway

SEATING

For entryway seating, select a timeworn bench or set of chairs with woven seats and a painted patina. Want to create a farmhouse patina on a yard sale piece? Start with a neutral base color and then layer in a palette of soft colors, such as faded blue and warm red. Dry brush on the contrasting colors, and then lightly sand and seal in the finish with a final coat of latex sealer.

TEXTILES

Go to textiles for the farmhouse look: flour sack fabric, burlap, linen, and ticking. Vintage aprons and linens are also a fun way to introduce farmhouse style to your entryway. Sew pillows from antique linens. Lightly tack vintage napkins to a ribbon to make a banner. Tie on strips of fabric to a throw and toss over a chair for the perfect farmhouse addition to your entry.

Transitional Style

If you are a transitional decorator at heart, this is the entryway for you. If mixing and matching different styles and family heirlooms and colorful pieces and one-of-a-kind lamps with chandelier pieces that sparkle and shine are your thing, here are a few transitional design elements to show off your personality in your entryway.

WALL ART

Transitional style is all about mixing and matching different styles to make them work. For example, in the entry you might pair a traditional rug with an eclectic piece of art made by your cousin's sister-in-law's best friend's aunt. Think outside the box when decorating an entryway in transitional style. Hang a bicycle on the wall or copy an oversized map of your hometown and frame it in smaller pieces to make a statement wall in the entryway.

STORAGE

Get creative with your organization. Repurpose one-of-a-kind pieces such as a vintage mail sorter into storage for your entryway. Add galvanized metal boxes for spare keys and papers, and hang desk drawers on the wall with hooks for purses and scarves. The key is to reimagine the purpose behind an item and rework it to fit your style.

RUGS

Oversized rugs with a large-scale pattern are often the foundation for transitional style. Mix and match patterns in the entry to create a transition from one style to the next. Kilim or Turkish rugs add layer and dimension to a space and introduce a brilliant color palette for this small space.

diy Stencil a bamboo mat with a favorite quote or scripture and then seal it with a latex topcoat. It's an easy way to add a little personality to your floor and your entryway.

SEATING

Colorful furniture with unusual texture is a perfect addition to any transitional entryway. Bamboo chairs, rattan chairs, painted wood pieces, and even vintage metal pieces add character and personality. Recover a chair seat with oilcloth or hand paint toile onto a yard-sale chair for a whimsical addition to the front entryway.

TEXTILES

Mix and match your textiles to create depth and personality in the entryway. Layer vintage fabric mixed with polka-dot cotton mixed with woven natural fiber materials. The more eclectic, the better. Add trim to pillows or tie tassels at the corner or even typography with a pillow featuring your favorite word of the year. Have fun and celebrate the style you love.

Contemporary Style

If you think you are a contemporary decorator at heart, this is the style for you. If clean lines and shiny surfaces and a little minimalism and bold colors mixed with leopard spots are your thing, here are a few contemporary design elements to show off your personality in your entryway.

WALL ART

Bold, graphic pieces work well in a contemporary entryway. Oversized abstract photographs or pop art matted in simple, clean-lined frames make a statement on the walls. Contemporary entryways have a minimalist feel, so make a bold statement with your art. A graphic piece, such as a large quote or scripture, printed on a white background and matted and framed in black is another budget-friendly option for the entryway. A grouping of mirrors in brilliant metallics or colorful sculpture work in the space as well.

STORAGE

Make storage fun. For example, red metal lockers are a fun way to visually pop a space. A live edge wood console brings an organic element juxtaposed to the clean lines and simplicity of contemporary design. Clear acrylic storage bins etched with labels are a creative way to organize keys, sunglasses, and other miscellaneous items by the front door.

RUGS

Bold, graphic patterns on the floor extend the contemporary style in a space. Choose black rugs with white polka dots or leopard print or a rug with contrasting stripes in vivid colors. In a contemporary entryway, you want to choose one element to truly provide graphic impact. If your rug makes a statement, make sure other elements of design are simpler to allow the rug to be the focus in the space.

SEATING

Contemporary seating features clean lines and unusual textures. Acrylic chairs with bold, graphic lines and leather and metal seating with grommets and nail heads are some fun options for the contemporary entryway. To maximize space, look for contemporary furniture that has more than one purpose. For example, choose a chair that doubles as a side table when the sides are folded. Dual-purpose furniture works well when space is at a premium.

TEXTILES

Make a statement with unusual materials and unusual pairings. Combine leather with sequins or leopard or faux fur pillows with taffeta. Textiles should be used sparingly in a contemporary space, so chose one area of design—windows, seating, or upholstery—to make a bold, graphic statement.

Coastal Style

If coastal decorating makes your heart smile, this is the entryway for you. If bleached white linens and light and airy colors and driftwood pieces turned into garlands make your heart sing, here are a few coastal design elements to show off your style in your entryway.

WALL ART

Adding coastal style to your walls is all about natural elements and artwork designed around a soothing color palette. Greet guests with an iconic beach scene or abstract watercolor in light blues and whites and creams and khakis that mimics the feeling of walking along the coastline. Frame coral or sand dollars on a linen background for interesting and unusual art pieces. Take your own photographs of beach scenes and frame them to add your own coastal personality to your walls. A vintage beach sign is also a fun piece to add to an entryway.

STORAGE

Coastal entryway storage is all about oversized baskets made from natural fiber, such as jute or hemp. Add oversized shells to your entryway table to hold keys and spare change, and place driftwood hooks just inside the door for coats or scarves.

 Make your own creative storage container. Start with a dollar store trash can and chunky rope. Wind the rope around the trash can and glue in place.

RUGS

Any rug placed in the front entry needs to be stylish as well as durable to hold up to sandy feet. Light and neutral rugs with a wide-open weave are the perfect solution. The color creates a welcoming feel to bare feet, and the weave allows the sand to fall through to the floor for easy cleanup.

SEATING

An entryway is the perfect place to add a pop of color with painted pieces. Repurpose a thrift store dresser with a stencil that mimics an inlay. Paint a chair in a light blue or a yellow or a cream and place it next to a basket by the front door. Distress painted pieces lightly with sandpaper to give furniture an added layer of depth and texture.

TEXTILES

Mimic the feeling of sand and sun and water with brightly colored patterned textiles. Mix in patchwork pieces and textured fabrics as well.

 Create your own pillows by copying vintage photographs onto fabric. Then sew the fabric into a one-of-a-kind coastal piece for your front entryway.

A Little Organization with Your Entryway

Organization starts at the entryway. Nothing says, "Welcome to my home" better than a little entryway organization. Even if the rest of the house has overflowing closets, an entire colony of socks assembling under the bed, and extra drawers collecting junk, if your entryway is organized, then your home looks as though an organizational rock star lives there.

The challenge? Most entryways are small. The space is typically at a premium. The solution? Making every square inch of the front entry work for you.

Here are a few creative organizational ideas to get started.

ORGANIZE YOUR DRAWER—Use drawer dividers (found at most big box stores) to create spaces in the drawer. Add a small bin for keys, extra coins, and miscellaneous items. Leave space for sunglasses, phones, and other necessities.

HANG IT UP—Put up a row of hooks just inside the entryway. This is a fun place to show off your personality. Make your own hooks with vintage silverware or decorative knobs or even a row of labeled pegs for each member of the family.

ADD A TRAY—Wet boots need a home, and what better place to store them than with a boot tray in the entryway? In winter months, place a scraper just outside the door, and then add a tray just inside the door for messy snow days.

TRY VERTICAL STORAGE—If your space is small, maximize your wall space with a shelf. Using brackets, hang a shelf above a row of hooks and add baskets for mittens, hats, scarves, and other outdoor accessories. In the summertime, you can store beach towels and outdoor toys in the baskets as well.

ADD AN EXTRA HOOK—I'm always leaving my purse all over the house, and then when I need it, it's hard to find. Solve this dilemma by hanging a small hook on a bookshelf or console. Now your purse will always have a home.

diy Create a faux entryway table. Place a 1" x 10" x 6' pine board on a set of pine legs (found in the molding section of the home improvement store). After you've determined the height, bolt the board to the wall and screw in the legs to the board. Place baskets for organization below the table and add a row of hooks above to maximize space.

CONTEMPORARY

Hello, joy. This contemporary entrance is designed to bring a smile to all who knock. From the matching set of pink doors to the crisp, white architectural features to the assortment of greenery, every element in this space is designed to brighten up the front porch. Matching wreaths on the doors, the sparkle of brass hardware, and the height of the oversized topiary add personality and life to the space. The signature contemporary piece? The plaid entry mat that brings the fun, anchors the space, and never takes itself too seriously.

TRADITIONAL

Adding traditional style to the front door, this textured grapevine wreath covered in layers of greenery mixed with natural elements provides a classic contrast to the brass pineapple plaque and burnished brass hardware.

COASTAL

This simple wreath made of sea grasses woven with jute on to a circular frame and topped with seashells welcomes guests and their sandy feet at the door of this beach home.

TRANSITIONAL

The brilliance and shine of a black door is brought to life with this lush wreath covered in sprigs of lamb's ear. Tied onto a satin nickel door knocker, the wreath says, "Welcome!" in a unique and creative way.

FARMHOUSE

Why use a traditional wreath when a creative farmhouse basket works so much better instead? This farmhouse front door features a woven basket filled with layers of individual succulent branches.

701

diy

Pineapple
Address Sign

Supplies

oval wood plaque

gold acrylic paint

white acrylic paint

black acrylic paint

small paintbrush

pineapple silhouette

carbon paper

pencil

house numbers printed
out on your home printer

100 grit sandpaper

water-based sealer

Instructions

1. Paint the wood plaque white. Let dry.

2. Place a piece of carbon paper over the plaque. Using the pencil, trace the pineapple silhouette on the painted plaque.

3. Paint the silhouette with gold paint. Let dry.

4. Using the same method of carbon paper and a pencil, outline your house numbers below the pineapple on the plaque.

5. Fill in with black paint. Let dry.

6. Distress with sandpaper.

7. Seal plaque with a water-based sealer.

The Living Room

Let Your Living Room (Not Your Couch) Do the Talking

I still remember my first living room in my first home.

When I worked on the design for the space, I planned it around a couch—ordered from an 8" x 8" fabric swatch at the furniture store. The fabric was bright yellow with giant blue and red and pink flowers scattered across its cushions. In the weeks leading up to the couch's arrival from the manufacturer, I painted the walls tomato red with brilliant white moldings, purchased a pink-and-white rug, and found two royal-blue-and-white patterned side chairs.

At the risk of stating the obvious, the room was going to be amazing.

Finally, after weeks of waiting, the couch arrived. The movers carried it inside, placed it on the rug, and unpacked the cardboard surround. They unwrapped first one arm and then the other until my couch was there in all its glory.

I stared at it in astonishment.

My eyes darted to the chairs and the rug and the walls—and in that moment one thought swirled around and around and around in my head.

WHAT WAS I THINKING?

What had looked like an incredible design choice on an 8" x 8" swatch was a hot mess in real life. The couch was so bright and floral and colorful and generally overwhelming that the rest of the room didn't stand a chance. What I thought would blend in, didn't. What I thought would be a colorful palette full of whimsy and fun, wasn't.

Not. Even. Close.

It was our first house. We didn't have the budget to change the design. So, I gritted my teeth, tried to make it all work, and eventually learned to live with it.

But that first living room taught me something.

It taught me that magazine clippings do not a room make. It taught me to think twice before ordering an expensive couch from a fabric swatch smaller than a piece of typing paper. It taught me that when selecting a large piece for a space, go neutral.

And let your space, not your couch, do the talking.

This chapter is all about living rooms and the people who love them.

Before we talk room style, before we take a look at different living rooms in different homes and discuss different styles, let's take a look at a few principles of living room design. If you are planning a living room redesign, here are a few tips to get you started.

Start with the Largest Upholstered Piece First

The biggest piece in your room typically determines what the rest of the room looks like. For example, once I went with my brilliant yellow couch, it didn't leave me a lot of wiggle room with design. Choosing a couch in a khaki or a gray or dark leather provides a foundation to build the rest of the room around. You can change your paint color and your pillows for under $100. But a couch? That's much more of an investment. Stay with a basic overall small pattern or solid to extend the design possibilities in your space.

Design an Arrangement for Conversation

If the living room is the heart of the home, then its seating arrangement is the heartbeat. People want to share their thoughts and dreams and stories. Design a room to accommodate that. Place upholstered pieces adjacent to each other. Group chairs together with a small table in between. Place a chair on either side of the couch. The key is to design a room for comfort and conversation. One quick tip for designing spaces is to place painter's tape on the floor to gain an overall perspective on the design. Measure each piece of furniture, and then outline it on the floor with tape to help your eye see the room visually before purchasing the furniture.

Be Intentional

Sometimes we are tempted to fill a space with stuff. We have extra furniture and extra wall space, and we place something on a wall or in a corner just because we think we have to. Don't. Every wall doesn't need to be filled. Every space doesn't need to have something in every corner. Let your room breathe. Make sure every piece of furniture has a function. When you fill your living room with things you love and things with a purpose, it will feel authentic and welcoming.

Place Furniture with a Purpose

If you take nothing else away from this chapter, remember this: Don't let your furniture be in a relationship with your walls. Pull it into the space. Pull it away from the wall. You will be surprised at how much difference it makes in a room. It gives the room movement and helps it feel purposeful and intentional.

Press Pause

Sometimes one of the most important things you can do for a space is simply live in it. We are often in such a rush to design a room that we overlook some of its basic functions. Live in the space. Watch where people sit. Do you need to add a small side table? Watch what the room is used for. Do you need to add a game table or a desk or another conversation area? Let the room dictate to you what it needs. Just be sure to listen.

Coastal Style
Q & A with KariAnne

A curve is at the top of the hill just before you get to our beach house. When I was younger, we'd drive two days across the country in an old blue station wagon full of crayons and pieces of paper and bent straws and petrified chicken nuggets.

It was a long haul.

Kids and suitcases and all the stuff our family needed for a month at the beach was piled high in the car. State by state passed by as we'd stare out the window at the passing scenery. Minutes turned into hours that turned into days.

And then?

Just when we thought we couldn't drive one more mile…just when we couldn't play one more game of license plate bingo…just when the crumbs and the paper and the pillows and the blankets were about to take over the car, we'd arrive at that curve.

And you could smell the ocean.

I was raised on the beach. I spent summers on the Cape Cod shore with the sand between my toes and the wind in my hair. I love sand dollars and starfish and anchors and sea horses and the smell of an ocean breeze. Here's a little more about me and my love for coastal style.

This is the super awkward part of the book where I interview myself about myself . . .

You are known for farmhouse style. Tell us a little about how it influenced your beach house design.

I think that farmhouse design and coastal design are first cousins. Both celebrate the organic, the authentic, and the surrounding countryside. They just have different perspectives. When I was designing this living room for our family's beach house, I added in farmhouse elements to the space. For example, the white bench under the window, the natural fiber rug in the space, the farmhouse chairs, and the whiteware are all nods to farmhouse design.

What one coastal element is a must-have?

I do love a piece of driftwood. There's just something about it that makes me smile. You can stand it alone or create art or functional pieces with it. I have a bowl sitting on the coffee table in my living room made of driftwood and a wreath in the bathroom made of driftwood. One of my favorite things to do is bring a piece of driftwood up from the beach and let it dry in the sun. The color is amazing.

 How does your faith influence your design?

I want to create a sanctuary in my home for my family. I want our home to honor God and serve as a buffer against a world that can be overwhelming at times. I want our home to restore them and give them strength. My desire is to design spaces where family and friends are welcome to share their hearts and their faith.

What's one way you could add a little coastal to a space for under $10?

Create your own artwork for your room. Take a simple piece of plywood from the home improvement store. Purchase chipboard letters and trace a quote or scripture onto the wood. Paint with an inexpensive acrylic craft paint and distress with sandpaper. Character, personality, and fun for your walls for under $10.

What's your favorite piece of furniture ever in the history of ever?

I have a hutch in my home I found at a yard sale years ago for $75. It was tucked away in the back of the garage and covered with tools and old paint. I fell in love with the lines and the tiny bits of architectural detail on the hutch. It's wide but super narrow, so it works in most spaces. I brought it home, cleaned it, dusted it off, and painted it (it's been several different colors). Years later it's still one of my favorite pieces.

A Coastal Living Room

Coastal style is all about blue skies, sunshine, sandy feet, summer breezes, and the first hint of the ocean at the top of the curve. Looking to add a little coastal to your design? Here are some design elements that will help introduce the beach into your living room.

DRIFTWOOD

If you live by the beach, you can find driftwood along the shoreline. It's full of texture and has a sculptural feel—use it in abundance. You can DIY your own driftwood wreath or garland. Paint driftwood with coastal colors, such as light blues, yellows, and creams, and fill a clear vase. A large piece of driftwood can stand alone. Place it on a bookcase or mantel as an organic piece of sculpture.

STRIPES, STRIPES, AND MORE STRIPES

Nothing says beach like a striped pattern. Choose a neutral palette with soft, warm colors such as khaki and cream, or go bold with a nautical palette of navy and white. Add stripes to the living room with oversized pillows and smaller upholstered pieces. Create striped roman shades for windows, or add a striped umbrella to the front porch.

NAUTICAL ELEMENTS

Add a little character and personality to your space with some creative nautical elements. The key is repurposing traditional nautical pieces in an unusual way. For example, paint stripes on oars or frame a grouping of life preservers to create a display on the living room wall. Glue starfish and sand dollars onto a piece of plywood and create an oversized flag for your space. Hang lobster buoys on hooks for color, and DIY a piece of art made from a variety of knots.

CORAL

One of the most beautiful ways to add a little coastal to your space is with coral. When God was designing the oceans, He decorated the seas with beautiful coral sculptures. Place a piece of sponge coral under a cloche on your bookcase, drape a stack of books with coral beads, add a grouping of branch coral to a side table, or frame a large piece of flat coral to hang on the wall.

RECLAIMED WOOD

Wood that has been distressed by the ocean makes the perfect material for projects with a coastal flair. Sketch a whale or a sea horse or a mermaid on a piece of reclaimed wood. Cut out and distress. Paint an oversized sign with a coastal theme on a piece of reclaimed wood. Transform a piece of wood into an anchor, a lobster, a crab, or even an oversized clock, and hang as wall art.

ORGANIC ELEMENTS

Look no further than the organic elements found on the beach. Dry grasses and weave them into a wreath for the mantle. Create a fun coffee table display with painted rocks. Paint different words on the rocks and have your guests arrange them into sentences. Decorate picture frames with shells, or paint the inside of shells with metallic paint and use them in small display containers. Collect sea glass and add to a glass vase with a bunch of fresh flowers.

COASTAL STYLE DETAILS

 1 A built-in bench anchors the space.

 2 Group chairs together for conversation.

 3 Add pops of blue and white.

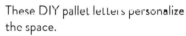 **4** A natural fiber rug grounds the space.

 5 Mix in textural elements, like this reclaimed wood mantel.

 6 These DIY pallet letters personalize the space.

 7 Vintage accessories keep the room authentic.

8 Start your own shell collection from walks on the beach.

9 Fresh flowers bring life to any coastal room.

Traditional Style

Yvonne's living room is timeless. Her furniture and accessories are carefully curated to create an overall classic design that has developed slowly, over time, with each piece intentionally chosen for the space. A classic sofa upholstered with neutral fabrics is paired with an antique coffee table and a pair of spindle armchairs. Her living room is full of texture and pattern, the patina of wood floors, and the traditional feel of vintage accessories. It's a lasting look that here's to stay. If traditional is your style, here are a few traditional design elements for your living room.

FURNITURE

Upholstered wingback chairs in damask or houndstooth are a perfect addition to a traditional style living room. Time-worn leather, with its soft patina and classic feel, works well in the space too. You could also keep all the upholstered pieces in the same color family to create a unified look to the room. Choose pieces intentionally, such as wood spindle-back chairs or a matching pair of antique side chairs. Glass-fronted bookcases filled with sets of classic books work well to anchor the space. Consider adding lighting to emphasize traditional pieces in the room as well as artwork.

FLOORING

Choose rugs for the space in rich, vibrant colors, with a thick pile that add to the feeling of timelessness in the space. Many traditional homes have hardwood floors, and vintage Oriental rugs are a great option. The purples and magentas of the patterns in the rugs highlight the rich patina of antique furniture in the space. A kilim rug is another choice to consider for the space. The traditional pattern of the rug creates a vivid foundation to design the rest of the room around.

FABRIC

When choosing fabrics for the traditional space, layer different types of patterns. Use the 60/30/10 rule. Select your favorite pattern for the space, and use it 60 percent of the time. Layer the next pattern 30 percent of the time, and lastly add in the remaining pattern 10 percent of the time. This general principle allows you to change the look of a space by varying the pattern. For example, if you choose the largest pattern for your 60 percent, the room will be bolder. If your 60 percent pattern is smaller, the room will be softer. Add in a few additional patterns, such as bold stripes or small polka dots, with pillows and other accessories in the space. Fabrics with small coastal elements, such as sea horses or crabs or anchors, work as well.

WINDOW COVERING

Traditional style window treatments are typically formal. Floor to ceiling drapes combined with roman shades or a valance create a traditional feel. Drapes are typically lined to add a classic feel to the room. You can change the look of a room by changing the density of color at the windows. For example, create a monochromatic look in the traditional style by continuing the color from walls to the window treatments in an overall pattern, such as a vertical stripe.

ACCESSORIES

This traditional living room features an oversized clock for the wall. Groupings of framed botanical prints or florals work as well in the space. Frame pieces in brass or metallic frames to add warmth and depth to displays. In addition, blue-and-white vases filled with fresh florals are the perfect accessory for a traditional mantel.

diy Print off a map of your local county or a place that holds special meaning. Take the map to a copy center and have it reproduced in a larger size. Cut and frame individual sections of the map to create a display for your walls.

Farmhouse Style

Walking into Bre's living room made me want to sink into the closest chair and put up my feet and never leave. Her rooms are full of grain-sack chairs lined up next to overstuffed, slipcovered couches with tiny side tables that look as though Farmer Brown built them in his barn. It's a put your feet up on the coffee table, a Scrabble game waiting to happen, and linens freshly scented with lavender kind of space. If farmhouse is your style, here are a few farmhouse design elements for your living room.

FURNITURE

When designing a farmhouse space, a slipcover is your friend. Typically, farmhouse furniture tends to be mismatched or oversized. A white, cream, or linen slipcover creates a feeling of unity in the space. Slipcovers are designed for comfort. They are tailored to the furniture and then adjusted with ties. Duck cloth or linen with ruffles and embroidered panels are designed to create a softer silhouette in the space.

FLOORING

Cover up those wide plank floors in the living room with oversized rugs in natural colors and textures. Many times, painted flooring is a great option for creating farmhouse style, and it's cost effective too. Instead of refinishing old, damaged floors, a coat of paint freshens a space for under $100. Paint a pattern on the floor or add a sea grass, jute, and sisal rug to the space. Layer natural fiber rugs with a smaller rug with a pop of pattern.

FABRIC

Layer fabrics in a variety of patterns and styles to help create the farmhouse look. Sew your own pillows for those slipcovered pieces in the space. Light blue or red ticking, linen, and grain sack all are durable options for pillow fabrics in the room. Look for vintage fabrics at yard sales and thrift stores that can be repurposed in your farmhouse space.

diy Create a simple cover for a side chair with flour sack fabric and ribbon. Cut a rectangular piece of fabric the approximate width of the chair. Hem on all four sides. Tack grosgrain ribbons on either side and tie onto the chair.

WINDOW COVERING

Window treatments in a farmhouse space are simple with clean lines. Tie unlined curtains to a rod or make your own inexpensive no-sew window treatments with drop cloths from the home improvement store. Most drop cloths come hemmed on all four sides. Use clips to clip the drop cloth to the curtain rod. Measure your windows to ensure the proper length for a hem. Allow four inches for the hem. Trim and iron in place with fusible iron-on tape.

ACCESSORIES

The chippier the better when it comes to farmhouse accessories. Frame artwork or family photos with vintage chippy frames made out of architectural salvage. Stack tall, painted baskets in different textures and patterns around the living room for additional storage. Add graphic quote signs, grapevine wreaths, galvanized metal pieces, woven striped throws, wood trays, and flat baskets for display on the coffee table. And the perfect farmhouse accessory? Fresh flowers, cut and arranged from the garden.

BY WISDOM A HOUSE
IS BUILT AND THROUGH
UNDERSTANDING IT
IS ESTABLISHED;
THROUGH KNOWLEDGE
ITS ROOMS ARE FILLED
WITH RARE AND
BEAUTIFUL TREASURES
PROVERBS 24:3

Transitional Style

Laura's living room is designed for celebrating family and creating a gathering place in the heart of her home. A striped chair and oversized sofas seated next to reclaimed wood pieces that have been handed down for generations make her transitional style living room feel warm and welcoming. It's a tell me about your day and grab a good book and listen to the classics play on a record player kind of style. If you are all about a room with a little transitional style, here are a few transitional design elements for your living room.

FURNITURE

Transitional style living rooms are designed for comfort. A mix of styles brings different elements of tradition and whimsy to the space. Many times, furniture in the room is handed down and treasured from generation to generation. Pieces aren't necessarily antiques; instead, they have meaning and sentimental value. A mix of wood, unusual finishes such as metal, painted patinas, and upholstered pieces give the room depth and character. The living room is designed for conversation. There is a table next to every upholstered piece and plenty of space to pull up a few chairs when guests arrive.

FLOORING

Transitional flooring in a space is a little eclectic. Transitional design is all about mixing styles, so flooring in a space can be anything from hardwood floors to tile to carpet. Adding a natural fiber rug to the existing flooring is a great way to ground the rest of the design. Or have fun and add a little personality to your space with a large rug with an overall pattern. If your upholstered pieces are neutral, add a little color with a graphic print or oversized, whimsical floral.

FABRIC

Transitional style is all about mixing and matching your fabrics in the room to add an eclectic feel to the space. Think outside the box when it comes to textiles. Add in textured fabrics with woven pillows with colorful patterns and designs. Select textiles with a story. Repurpose dish towels or vintage fabrics from your grandmother's linen collection into one-of-a-kind pieces for your living room.

diy Take a needlepoint or cross-stitch piece—one you create yourself or one handed down from your family. Stitch it onto the center of an existing pillow cover. Fill with a down pillow insert and stuff. It's a fun way to add a little bit of history to your space.

WINDOW COVERING

Window treatments in a transitional space are unique. Many times, transitional spaces will forgo window treatments in lieu of plantation shutters or simple pull-down privacy shades. The windows are designed to highlight the space by letting light into the room. Other times, a roman shade is used in place of floor-to-ceiling drapes. You can make your own roman shade with a drop cloth for an affordable window treatment option.

ACCESSORIES

Accessories in a transitional space come in a variety of patinas and textures. Hang a galvanized wreath on a barn door next to a wall of family photos and quotes. Fill a small bowl with vintage game piece accessories and place on a brass tray. Fill a whiteware pitcher with flowers and place it atop a stack of books on a vintage side table. Decorate a bookshelf with a graphic element, like a piece of sculpture next to a shiny brass tray filled with brightly colored architectural pieces.

> **TOTAL DECORATING ASIDE:** Decorate with conversation starters. I once framed a piece of molding just to keep it around for all the stories.

Contemporary Style

Carmel's style shines brightly in her contemporary living room. She flawlessly mixes furniture styles with current trends and layers in vivid, graphic punches of color. For example, she adds a pop of bold pattern to her neutral sofa with black-and-white striped pillows. A sculptural wire end table sits next to a contemporary leather sofa with a modern white coffee table in front. If contemporary is your style, here are a few design elements for your living room.

FURNITURE

Celebrate clean, classic lines with a minimalistic feel combined with texture and pattern in a contemporary living room. Repurpose furniture in a unique and creative way. Replace a coffee table with a red velvet bench. Let organic wood side tables made from tree stumps double as seating. Add a clear acrylic chair as both additional seating and a place to stack books and magazines when not in use. Repurpose, reuse, and rethink to create the contemporary look.

FLOORING

Hello, fun. Rethink traditional rugs and opt instead for graphic rugs with a bold, contemporary design. Juxtapose area rugs with vivid colors against the simplicity of furniture and accessory choices in the room. Leopard prints and animal prints as well as the clean lines of an overall graphic design all work in a contemporary space.

tip If you go bold with the rug, allow the eye to rest with lighter furniture selections for the design.

FABRIC

Group different types of patterns and colors together. Floor pillows are a fun and creative way to add in color to the space. Choose oversized pillows in polka dots or stripes or even velour. Stack pillows throughout the space for additional seating and visual interest. A few graphic textiles are all you need to make a statement in a contemporary space. Choose wisely, and let your stripes do the talking.

WINDOW COVERING

Window treatments are typically minimalistic or understated in a contemporary room. Simple white sheers work well to let in light and provide privacy. Add unusual trims to the window treatments, such as a ribbon with a Greek key design, small pompoms, or even monochromatic ruffles. Pull-down roller shades are also a great option.

 diy Create your window covering by transforming off-the-rack shades with a painted design or vinyl artwork.

ACCESSORIES

Think bold and unusual when you are thinking accessories for the living room. Choose colorful geodes on stands to decorate your bookcase and graphic typography for the walls.

Layer texture with brass sculptures and groupings of succulent plants. Lastly, add whimsy with a vintage collection of corks in a glass lamp or the character of a vintage typewriter.

 DIY a tray for the coffee table with a painted gold design and brass hardware.

NO WHINING
NO COMPLAINING
ABSOLUTELY
NO FROWNING
ONLY
HUGS, SMILES
and
WARM FUZZY FEELINGS
ARE ALLOWED

Thank you

COASTAL

If you listen closely to a coastal mantel, you can almost hear the sea. This reclaimed wood beam looks as if it might have washed ashore with the Mayflower and been carried up from the beach by Pilgrims. The character of the wood allows the whitewashed brick to take center stage. The mantel is then offset by the oversized wooden fish.

Just like the simplicity and ease of beach life, the mantel accessories are kept to a minimum. Stacks of covered books are grouped together for a casual feel. Lastly, items collected on trips to the beach are tucked atop books.

CONTEMPORARY

Bold, graphic artwork brings style in vivid hues with this contemporary mantel. Let the artwork shine and keep the mantel display simple with a pair of candlesticks, patterned candles, and a carved bowl full of texture.

FARMHOUSE

Farmhouse style is all about the chippy, distressed, and repurposed. Start with an oversized basket hung on the wall with a ribboned wreath. Next, whiteware pieces and distressed wood elements bring the farmhouse style.

TRANSITIONAL

Add authenticity to a transitional mantel with a little history. Here, vintage bowling pins and reclaimed wood pieces are layered against the chalkboard backdrop. Finish off the mantel with fresh greenery.

TRADITIONAL

Blue and white is a staple of most traditional mantels. Group porcelain vases or figurines next to traditional style lamps. Add shutters for height and a small white vase full of greenery to make the mantel pop.

diy

Magnolia
Wreath

1 HOUR   SKILL LEVEL

Supplies

faux magnolia leaves
Styrofoam wreath base
ribbon

TOTAL CRAFT ASIDE:
This craft can also be done
with real magnolia leaves.
Simply follow the same
directions, spritz them
with water every couple of
days, and your wreath
should last about
three to four weeks.

Instructions

1. Clip your faux magnolia leaves off the branch.

2. Start by inserting the first magnolia leaf into the foam base.

3. Stagger another leaf next to the first. Continue adding leaves until the foam base is completely covered. Make sure all the leaves are inserted in a clockwise direction so the wreath lies flat.

4. Hang up the wreath with a ribbon and use it to decorate a mirror or shutter or sign.

The Dining Room

3

When Your Table Is Ready to Party

I still remember when I told the dining room goodbye.

My mother had sold the house I grew up in, and I was on a farewell tour. Sobbing, I walked from room to room. I whispered goodbye to the bedroom with the Laura Ashley wallpaper and the empty closet that had held my collection of stirrup pants and prairie skirts. I waved to the staircase I had tromped down for decades. I silently nodded farewell to the mirror where I had stood on my wedding day in hot rollers and red lipstick before I left for the church. *And then?*

It was the dining room's turn.

I opened the antique French doors and closed my eyes and let the yesterdays flood into my heart. All the family dinners, all the special occasions, all the brunches and tea parties and celebrations. All the Thanksgivings. All the times I wished my mother would forget to serve brussels sprouts. Slowly and tearfully, with a heavy heart, I packed up the memories and closed the doors.

And walked away.

I thought that was the end. And then? Incredibly, inexplicably, amazingly, an opportunity arrived I never could have imagined. Months later I had called up the new owners and explained who I was and that I grew up in the home they had purchased from my mother. I went on to tell them that due to family circumstances, we would be moving back to the Dallas area, and would they, could they, might they…

…think about selling?

To my surprise, they said yes. God's timing was perfect. Just as He had made the way for the first jump to our farmhouse in Kentucky, He cleared the way to bring us home. Their house wasn't on the market yet, but they were being transferred and needed to sell. I couldn't believe it. And so it was that nine months later, on a sunny summer afternoon, we walked through the doors of that childhood home.

As its new owners.

It was all a little surreal. We started renovating immediately. We tore down the wall between the kitchen and the butler's pantry. There was new flooring, and the cabinets were reworked, and the walls and trim were painted, and new countertops were installed. My grandmother's chandelier sparkled over a new dining room table. Everything was ready. Everything was set.

Just in time for Christmas Eve.

We invited both our families over to celebrate the season. Plates piled high with food made their way into the dining room as the family gathered around the table. Laughter filled the air as we shared stories and memories sprinkled with joy. A new beginning. A new chapter. A new celebration—right where it all began.

Without any brussels sprouts.

That's what a dining room is all about. Whatever the style, whatever the design, all dining rooms have one common denominator—a place to gather and celebrate with family and friends. Before we take a look at different dining rooms designed in different styles, let's begin with a few principles of dining room design. If you are planning a dining room redesign, here are a few tips to get you started.

Lighting

One of the most important elements for creating drama and mood in a space is lighting. Start with a lighting fixture hung over the dining room table. To determine the approximate size of your over-the-table lighting fixture, simply measure the width and length of the room, add together, and change to inches. Sound confusing? Here's an example to explain a little better. If the room measures 12' x 12', add 12 + 12 = 24. Change 24' to 24", and that's the approximate size of the fixture you should choose.

Storage

Dining rooms come with plates and cups and bowls and glasses, and all of that dishware and glassware needs a place to park until it's time to party. Add a hutch or buffet with doors and drawers to a dining room to have a place to tuck in all those extra place settings and leave your table clutter free.

Extra Seating

Create an expandable version of your dining room to accommodate larger crowds. Make sure to purchase a dining table with a leaf, and place extra seating against a wall in your room.

tip Foldable metal chairs are a great option for additional seating. Cover with washable slipcovers that can be stored away until needed again.

Select the Right Rug for the Space

When selecting a rug for the dining space, go big or go home. You want to make sure your area rug covers enough of the room. A good rule of thumb is to allow at least 24" of space on either side of the dining table. This allows guests to have enough room to pull chairs up to the table. A rug pad is a great choice for a dining room rug to give extra cushion and help keep the rug in place.

Mix It Up a Little

Some people feel that a dining space has to be serious and stuffy and proper. Why not create a dining space that works for your family and your gatherings? Use your dining room every day instead of just for special occasions. Pull up a bench for extra seating. Pull up mismatched chairs to the table to give the room personality. Add pillows to chairs to create a room that says, "Make sure to stay for coffee and conversation after dinner."

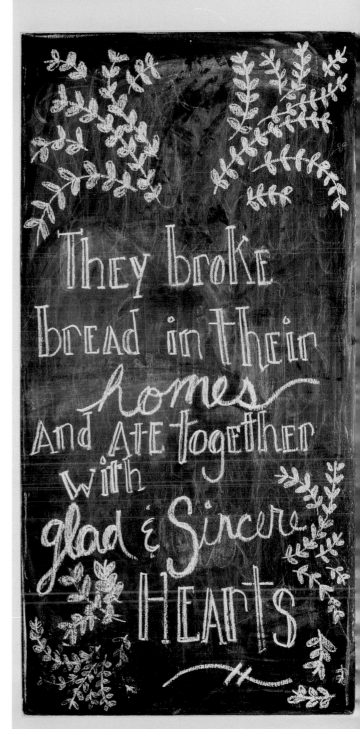

They broke bread in their homes And ate together with glad & sincere Hearts

Traditional Style Q & A with Yvonne

In the middle of photographing Yvonne's house, there was a moment I'll never forget. We had just finished styling the dining room. There were big containers full of fresh flowers from the yard in the middle of the table, and black-and-white dishes layered with vintage silver next to a grouping of oversized mercury glass candlesticks. Every detail was perfect. Every line of the linen khaki bench was in place.

Never had a dining room been more well behaved.

I grabbed a cup of coffee, sank into one of the chairs, and sighed with contentment. And then? Yvonne made me laugh. Not just a little laugh—the kind of laugh where you giggle so hard you throw your head back and holler with pure delight. And right there in the middle of that perfect dining room, joy opened up the door and walked in.

That's Yvonne.

That's the spaces she creates.

I think that's the secret behind using traditional elements to decorate a space like a dining room. You build a foundation of clean, classic design in the space. You layer neutrals and colors and furniture with brilliant patina and timeless pieces. And then? You add your own creative spin to truly make it yours.

Because Yvonne's father was in the military, she was raised in Scotland and England. She spent two years at a Scottish boarding school in a castle in Edinburgh, which helped shaped her perspective on design. She loves down pillows, oversized clocks, and blue-and-white dishes, and she never met a vignette she didn't like. Here's a little more about Yvonne and her love for traditional style.

Q What one traditional element is a must-have?

I am all about a covered book. I cover books and use them as risers or stack them as pillars to create a vignette. The texture is amazing, and they don't need to be the star. They are the perfect supporting characters. Nothing makes a better riser than three books covered in burlap.

Q What design books are on your bookshelf?

On my bookshelf, I have books from Charles Faudree and Bunny Williams. The design books I own don't necessarily have to be traditional styles. I love to collect books from all styles to see how other creatives decorate their homes. I think it's important to discover how other designers approach their rooms and what motivates them to design their spaces.

Q What is one thing you like to splurge on?

Can I have two? I have a set of linen sheets that literally changed my life. I'm a tactile person, and the feel of linen is so lofty and luxurious. I know this sounds funny, but I feel as if my linens know me. Fresh flowers are another splurge I love. There's no problem in the world that a vase of white tulips can't make a little better.

Q What's your favorite design tip?

Decorate a home for you and who lives in it. Don't decorate it according to the latest style. This is your home. This is your place. Learn what you love and what you don't. Learn what you can live with and what you can't. Decorate your sanctuary to reflect you.

Q What is one piece of advice you would give to someone about decorating?

Learn from your mistakes. I have learned more from my mistakes than I have from anything else. Everyone is so afraid to make mistakes, and then they get stuck. They want a beautiful home, but they are so afraid they will choose the wrong thing. Sometimes the only way we learn is by doing.

A Traditional Dining Room

Do you have a dining room that needs a little updating? Looking to add traditional elements to your design? Here are some specific things to create a timeless, classic feel to your space.

FLORAL ARRANGEMENTS

When accessorizing a dining with traditional elements, oversized floral arrangements are a staple. When creating a centerpiece for the dining room table, start with a beautiful urn or blue-and-white porcelain container. Next, add in dried or faux floral stems to create height and drama. Fill the rest of the arrangement with texture. Add in feathers or branches or bunches of greenery.

OIL PAINTINGS

Nothing says timeless style like the beautiful depth and patina of a classic oil. Still-life paintings of fruit or flowers in ornate gold frames make a statement on the walls. Portrait paintings done in oil are another classic addition to the space. Add your own family history, or purchase a little history at the thrift store.

SYMMETRY

There's something about symmetry that makes a space feel timeless. Two paintings, two chairs, two vases all work to create harmony in the space—especially with dining room tables, side boards, or mantels. Balance out both sides of the display with similar objects at the same height. Create a seamless look using similar materials with the vignettes.

TAILORED LINENS

In a traditional dining space, linens are typically tailored with seamstress detailing. For example, select a table runner with pleating and cording. Placemats in luxurious fabrics should be hemmed and starched for a more formal feel. Fabric napkins are a great option for the table. Add a monogram and napkin ring, and your table is ready to party.

TASSELS

The traditional dining room is the place where all the tassels come to live. Tassels come in all shapes and sizes. Often, the top part of the tassels resembles a piece of art. There are tassels with wood-carved tops, tassels with gilded tops, and tassels with ornate, hand-painted scenes. Don't skimp on tassels. Instead, choose rich, luxurious materials, such as heavy cotton or silk cording. Use them to tie back curtains, add them to pillows or trim a lamp.

6

9

1. A traditional buffet is perfect for dining room storage.

2. A slipcovered bench adds tailored style with traditional flair.

3. Use a large tureen filled with fresh flowers as a centerpiece.

4. An oversized mirror reflects the natural light from the windows.

5. Add a rug large enough to accommodate the dining table and chairs.

6. Let architectural elements on windows shine.

7. Group mercury glass candlesticks in varying heights around the centerpiece.

8. A drum shade chandelier with a ceiling medallion adds light and sparkle to the room.

9. Upholstered wingback chairs anchor the seating in the space.

Farmhouse Style

When I was younger, we went to visit an Amish farmhouse for dinner. The furnishings were simple. The table was made out of pine boards and sat 20 people end to end in mismatched chairs with rush seats. Each place setting had a simple white plate, a fork, a knife, and a spoon. But the star of the show was the food. The table was filled to the brim with dishes and bowls and platters piled high with fresh fruits, vegetables, and home-made bread still steaming from the oven.

That's dinner—farmhouse style. Want to add a little farmhouse and some fresh green beans to your dining room table? Here are some style tips to get you started.

FURNITURE

The foundation of any farmhouse dining room is the table. Farmhouse tables are typically oversized and made from white oak or pine. The bigger the table, the more guests to invite. Chairs are usually wood with slatted or decorative backs. Have fun with farmhouse furniture. Mismatch the chairs. Hang the leaf from the table on the wall as a decorative accent. Create a display piece for the space by stacking an open hutch on a sideboard. Choosing pieces with character and style adds authenticity and coziness to your dining room.

LINENS

Many times, linens in a farmhouse dining room have a story to tell. Purchase vintage linens at thrift stores and estate sales. Look for monogrammed linens to add personality to your table. Use linens for place mats and chair covers. DIY a liner for a tray or basket out of a vintage dish towel. Sew a quick hem, thread a ribbon through the hem, and tie onto the edge of the basket. When not in use, display stacks of linens on your hutch or in an oversized farmhouse basket.

DISHES

Simple white dishes work best in a farmhouse dining space and can be found at yard sales for less than a dollar. Mix and match patterns in different place settings. Fill the hutch in the dining room with pieces of milk glass or a collection of luncheon plates. Blue-and-white china is another fun addition to the farmhouse dining table. A few pieces mixed in with white dishes create a clean, classic look for a place setting.

CENTERPIECE

Keep it simple when planning a farmhouse centerpiece, and decorate with the scents and textures of the outdoors. Place a large basket in the center of the table, and fill it with boxwood and ivy and other greenery. Or create a grouping of milk glass vases in the center of the table, and fill them with fresh flowers from the garden. Even a simple display, like a bowl of apples or other fresh fruit, makes a simple centerpiece for the table.

LIGHTING

A single light fixture over the table adds a soft ambiance to the farmhouse table. Choose a chandelier with vintage flair in sparkling crystals and polished brass accents. Or go all-industrial farmhouse with a light fixture created from organic elements, like a wine barrel chandelier made from bent wood with metal accents. For a special occasion, why not move the farmhouse table out into the backyard and dine by the best light of all? Candlelight.

> **TOTAL DECORATING ASIDE:** If you can't find a farmhouse frame, make one of your own. Especially if you have some wood with attitude.

Transitional Style

My grandmother was a trendsetter. She loved color, texture, and pattern, and her china looked as if it came directly from Coco Chanel's table. The dishes were magenta and turquoise and brilliant yellow with tiny swirls and stripes and edged with gold leaf. Even the teacups were pieces of art. From the tiny bent handle to the matching saucer. That china was a sight to behold. My mother inherited that set of china, and when she set the table with those dishes, you felt as though royalty was coming to dinner.

That's dinner—transitional style. Want to add a little transitional and some royal decrees to your dining room table? Here are some style tips to get you started.

FURNITURE

Planning a dining space set in transitional style is a lot like getting married. There's a little old, a little new, and a whole lot of family. Layer the dining furniture into the space—pieces that have been handed down from generation to generation. The key to this style is decorating with what you love. For example, start with a dining room table that was handed down to you for sentimental reasons. Don't have chairs that match? No worries. Combine the table with upholstered pieces or a set of mid-century modern chairs. Add in a farmhouse hutch. The mix of styles works because it is uniquely you.

LINENS

Transitional design is all about creating a unified look from different styles. Have fun with your textiles. Start with chargers you just found at a thrift store, layer expensive linen placemats you got as a wedding present, and finish off the look with vintage monogrammed napkins from your grandmother. You don't necessarily have to match all your linens. Simply add in patterns and colors that work together in the dining space.

DISHES

Just like my grandmother's china, dishes in a transitional style place setting are typically eclectic. Combine two or more patterns on the table to add character and personality to each guest's place. Think outside the box when it comes to chargers for the transitional table. Use vintage cutting boards or grapevine wreaths or even heirloom round silver trays to add personality and character to each place setting.

diy Create your own napkin rings from vintage silver plate. Flatten the head of a spoon and stamp it with initials or the name of your guest. Bend the spoon in a circle, and then tuck the napkin inside. Guests can take their napkin rings home as a party favor.

CENTERPIECE

Create a fun and unique centerpiece for the transitional table by repurposing everyday items. Place a shutter in the center of the table as a runner and line it with potted plants. Line up chalkboards along the center of the table. Write encouraging messages or scripture on the chalkboards, and add mason jars filled with fresh flowers. Fill a toolbox with tiny vases of hydrangeas or peonies and place in the center of the table.

LIGHTING

Lighting in a transitional space comes in many different patterns and textures. Hang a chandelier made of metal and wood beads to visually fill the space over the table. Or choose a crystal chandelier encased in an oversized drum shade or maybe a square metal chandelier with clean lines and graphic design. The key is choosing a fixture you love and making it work in your space.

Contemporary Style

I love New York. It's full of brilliant places and brilliant museums and brilliant restaurants. I once walked through the doors of a restaurant that looked as if it had stepped out of the pages of a Broadway play. There were graphic steel columns, walls of glistening glass, and rows and rows of gold velvet upholstery with brown-and-cream-striped velvet pillows. On the ceiling was a fixture of lighted branches, and each table had a starched white linen cloth and sparkling crystal glasses.

That's dinner—contemporary style. Want to add a little contemporary and some Broadway to your dining room table? Here are some style tips to get you started.

FURNITURE

Contemporary style is all about clean lines with a trendy feel. Choose minimalistic furniture, such as a table with a glass top and metal legs or a reclaimed wood table with a live edge or a simple white table with acrylic edging. Dining chairs should have a contemporary feeling as well. Choose open-back, graphic metal chairs or brilliantly patterned chairs with pops of color or overstuffed armchairs with a unique silhouette.

LINENS

Linens for the table should be graphic with a bold, contemporary design. Choose bright patterns in black and white or vivid pops of colors. Create a unique look for your table with an ombré table runner or round mesh place mat. Select linens for the table in creative patterns, such as faux bois, zebra, or leopard. Lastly, layer linens made from natural materials, such as rattan, natural fibers, or jute.

DISHES

Let your dishes shine when it comes to setting your contemporary table. Add bowls and plates in solid colors with different sheens. For example, mix matte plates with shiny bowls and finish the place setting with metallic chargers. Don't forget to bring the pattern too. Layer polka dots with stripes with tiny prints and swirls. A contemporary table never met a patterned dish it didn't like.

diy Create your own graphic statement with message plates. Start with a clear glass plate. Print out a word or saying in reverse on vinyl. Add to the back of the clear plate and set one at each place setting.

CENTERPIECE

Create a colorful centerpiece for your table with graphic, colorful vases. Set a grouping of narrow-stemmed vases in the center of the table, and add a single brilliantly colored stem to each vase. Fill an oversized metal-and-glass vase with several sculptural flower stems, such as calla lilies or dahlias. Or create an arrangement of monochromatic colors in the same color family for a centerpiece with vivid impact.

LIGHTING

Brilliantly bold lighting fixtures are the perfect design for a contemporary space. Hang a brushed nickel-plated starburst with miniature twinkling lights over the dining room table. Select a contemporary styled white flower pendant for its sculptural design and graphic silhouette. Or choose an oversized black drum shade lined with gold for drama and sophistication in your contemporary dining room.

> **TOTAL DECORATING ASIDE:**
> If a tree falls in the forest, some people wonder what kind of noise it makes. I wonder how many side tables I can make from it.

Coastal Style

On the shores of Cape Cod Bay, when the sun would start to set and brilliant rays of light danced across the sand, you'd find my family down at the beach around a campfire. We'd have cookouts and picnics with fresh seafood and corn on the cob with the ocean breezes rippling across the water. When the stars came out, we'd roast marshmallows and make s'mores with chocolate dripping across the sand.

That's dinner—coastal style. Want to add a little coastal and some fresh ocean breezes to your dining room table? Here are some style tips to get you started.

FURNITURE

A distressed pine table or even a white painted wood table helps to provide a foundation for coastal style in the dining room. The key to bringing a beachy feel to the space is to bring the outdoors in. Keep colors in the space light and breezy with neutral tones or in light colors, such as khaki, blue, and white. Light walls provide a backdrop for comfortable, casual wood furniture. Rattan chairs or bamboo pieces bring an element of texture and coastal flair to the dining room.

LINENS

Create an airy, beachy feeling in the dining room with light, sun-washed fabrics. Keep the table linens simple with bleached white place mats and a blue-and-white striped runner. Soft colors such as khaki and cream work well in a coastal setting. Mix in vintage beach-themed fabrics for a dining room that doesn't take itself too seriously.

 Make your own coastal chargers. Start with a circle cut from cardboard. Using heavy jute twine, start at the center of the circle and wind the rope clockwise until the cardboard circle is covered. Glue the rope down as you wind it on the cardboard. Cut the last of the piece of rope at a slant and glue the end in place. The texture of the rope provides the perfect beachy accent for your table.

DISHES

Start with basic white dishes, and then add pattern and fun to your place settings with pops of color. Layer polka dots with striped with swirls. Cornflower blue and white work well as a traditional beach palette. The colors bring in the sea and the sun. But why not have a little bit of fun? Dial up the color a little with hot pink and yellow and orange. Dishes are an easy and inexpensive way to add a little color and personality to the table.

CENTERPIECE

Create a centerpiece for your coastal table in minutes. Place a grouping of glass vases in the center of the table, and fill them with shells and add fresh flowers. Or create a centerpiece from an oversized piece of driftwood. Place the driftwood on a tray and glue starfish to the wood to add visual interest. Another easy and fun idea is to fill a container with sand and place shells and sea glass and sand dollars hidden in the sand. Place a small sand shovel at each guest's place setting and encourage them to dig for buried treasure.

LIGHTING

When choosing lights for a coastal dining room, select a fixture that adds organic texture and shimmer and shine to the space. For example, an open chandelier created from oyster shells adds coastal style with organic elements. Woven rope fixtures created entirely from sea knots or a brilliantly colored light fixture made from turquoise sea glass brings the feel of sunshine and sand and ocean breezes to the dining room.

FARMHOUSE

Place settings are a fun way to let your personality pull up a chair to the table. Mix and match patterns and colors with dishes and textiles. Add farmhouse style with an oversized check pattern layered with crisp white linens and the subtle, soft hue of dyed-blue napkins. Use woven chargers or even wood slices to add an organic element.

Farmhouse style is all about a simple and no-fuss table. Add a pop of color to the table with vintage blue glassware and flowers from the garden. Wrap napkins in jute twine, and use pieces of driftwood as a place cards.

TRADITIONAL

This traditional place setting starts with a white charger with raised scrollwork. Brilliantly patterned black-and-white dishes are set at each place with a cup full of fresh hydrangea. Mercury glass brings a shine to the table.

CONTEMPORARY

Nothing says contemporary style like leopard plates mixed with colorful blue and red dishes. Simple white dishes and metal chargers allow the vivid patterns of the more colorful dishes to take center stage.

TRANSITIONAL

A little shine, a little blue, a little vintage, and a little new. A copper vase with blue hydrangea brings color to the table. Simple white dishes, black-and-white textiles, and chalkboard place cards celebrate transitional style.

COASTAL

Blue-and-white textiles layered with jute place mats add coastal style to this antique oak table. Classic silverware, blue-and-white dishes, and a glass vase filled with shells and fresh flowers add the airy, breezy style.

Supplies

decorative white plate
ceramic marker

Instructions

1. This is one of my family's favorite traditions. Start by placing the plate at the place setting of the guest of honor at any celebration. We use the plate for birthdays and anniversaries and dance recitals and baseball games and anything and everything that we celebrate.

2. Have the guest of honor initial and write the reason for the celebration and the date on the back of the plate for that celebration with the ceramic marker. Keep adding signatures and dates to the back of the plate. It's a fun way for family and friends to remember all the celebrations that have gone before.

The Kitchen

The Heartbeat
of the Home

Years ago, I stood at my kitchen door and broke up with my boyfriend just before he left for boot camp. I hugged him tight and wished him well. Then I shut the door and turned away with tears in my eyes and resolution in my heart.

Breaking up with each other was for the best.

He was nice and sweet and kind with twinkling brown eyes, but I had big plans. BIG. I was 21 with a prairie skirt and concho belt and high heels with lace socks and a life planned out down to the last detail. I didn't have time for distractions or boot camps or sailors or twinkling eyes.

But then I'd hear a joke or a funny story that only a pair of twinkling eyes would understand. And somewhere between 27 bites of chocolate and daytime television and crying myself to sleep, I realized I was totally, hopelessly, irrevocably in love with the sailor I just broke up with.

It was terrible. I couldn't let him know. There wasn't a cell phone or internet or email or a way to tell someone that you had totally changed your mind and you never wanted to be away from them again and you would follow them to the ends of the earth.

And back again.

A month later the phone rang. It was him—just calling to tell me he was thinking of me. He'd waited an hour in line at the pay phone to talk to me, and he knew I was probably busy, but he missed me.

I said nothing.

I wanted to, but I was sobbing. I sank to the floor of the kitchen and dissolved into a puddle of tears. I couldn't believe he called me. I couldn't get the words out that I wanted to say. So my heart spoke for me. On a cold, gray, February morning on a pay phone with a tender note in his voice, a sailor told a girl he loved her.

And she told him she loved him right back.

Kitchens always have the best love stories. Perhaps because they are the heartbeat of the home. It's probably safe to say that whatever design style your kitchen is, it's the center of your home's universe. Kitchens are the gathering place, the homework place, the bake-an-apple-pie-when-you're-sad kind of place, the twirl-until-you're-dizzy kind of place, and the place where all the stories start.

Before we take a look at different kitchens from the perspective of each design style, let's begin with a few principles of kitchen design.

Organization

Kitchens come with lots of stuff. There are pots and pans and mixers and measuring cups and blenders. The key to falling in love with your kitchen is to find a place for everything and keep everything in its place. In our kitchen at the farmhouse, there was one giant drawer that held an entire army of kitchen supplies. I'd spend hours digging through thermometers and whisks and apple corers just to find a measuring cup. When we remodeled our kitchen at the new house, there are now a series of tiny drawers on one side of the island, and one holds measuring spoons and cups. No more searching and digging.

The measuring cup is now just a tiny drawer away.

Keep your kitchen organized in style with simple organizing tips like these: Simplify drawers with organizers. Place pot lids on a kitchen organizer that hangs on the cupboard door. Fill baskets with plastic plates and cups and napkins for unexpected guests. Stack spices in the cabinet on risers. Create an entire family command center on the back side of a cabinet door with peel-and-stick chalkboards and calendars.

Kitchen Triangle

During a kitchen remodel or when updating appliances, it's important to keep the kitchen triangle in mind to maximize efficiency in the space. Typically, there are three work centers in a kitchen: the stove, the refrigerator, and the sink. Place each of these elements in the space so that they form a triangle. This allows the cook to easily travel from one area of the space to another in the most efficient manner when preparing a meal.

Kitchen Zones

Because the kitchen is the center of the home, many different activities take place in this space. When redesigning a kitchen, plan a space or zone for each one. For example, in our home the kitchen is used for homework and as an after-school retreat. Meals are prepared in the kitchen, and we need a place to grab a quick snack or eat breakfast in the morning.

Each activity takes place in a specific zone. Homework is zoned for the kitchen bar area. The main kitchen triangle is used to prepare meals, and bar stools are added to the island for a quick snack.

Labels

One simple way to reduce chaos in the kitchen is to use labels. Dozens of free downloadable label templates are available online. Design specific labels for your kitchen, print them out, and use them to help organize your space. For example, in our kitchen, I have my shelves, my pantry area, my drawers, and my cleaning supply spaces all labeled. Using labels also helps me when making a list for the grocery store. I just look at the blank spaces next to the labels to see what the kitchen needs more of.

Pantry Organization

The pantry can either be the kitchen's best friend or its worst nightmare. Truth? If the pantry is happy, then everyone is happy. I use baskets with labels in my pantry to maximize space and sort food into categories. I have a basket for snacks, a basket for breakfast items, a basket for chips, a basket for things I use for baking, and so on. Add additional storage space with vertical storage on the doors and hanging baskets that slide onto shelves.

Farmhouse Style
Q & A with Bre

We arrived on a bright summer day to photograph Bre's house in coastal New Hampshire. As our car tires crunched on the gravel driveway, a soft breeze created a flutter across the brilliantly colored countryside. I slowly climbed out of the car with the warm sunshine on my face, and then, suddenly, there was Bre. She greeted us with a smile and a wave. She was barefoot with rolled-up jeans and a casual, breezy shirt, carrying a bucketful of chicken food. And then?

The chickens came running.

Pecking and flapping and clucking, they arrived at the party. Bre greeted them and called them by name as she scattered the food across the meadow. Each chicken had a personality, she explained. *Sunshine* has white feathers with a topknot. She's a cuddler. She's dainty and delicate and loves to be held. *Snuggles* has red feathers and a bossy personality. She's the top of the chicken-pecking order. The queen bee. The leader of pack. *Tyson,* has black feathers, and she's a fighter. She's tough and fierce

and full of extra chicken spunk.

The flock circled us as Bre made the introductions. The experience was incredible. Everywhere I looked, I was inspired. The farmhouse was warm and welcoming. The air was full of sunshine and the smell of fresh grass. I wanted to kick off my shoes and pull up a chair on the front porch with a glass of sweet tea and spend the afternoon with the meadow and the chickens.

That's Bre and her home.

That's the casual, breezy feeling of farmhouse style.

She loves white slipcovers, grain-sack fabric, barn wood, and galvanized metal, and she believes every flower arrangement needs a maple syrup bucket. Here's a little more about Bre and her love for farmhouse style.

How does farmhouse style influence your design?

I want my farmhouse style to look and feel relaxed and inviting. For me, it's not so much about specific individual elements of farmhouse design; it's more about creating a feeling. I don't want my rooms to feel stiff or formal. Instead, I want the spaces in my home to feel casual and warm and welcoming. I love to create spaces that invite people to come in and stay.

What are your favorite stores to shop at?

I wish I had a super fancy shopping answer for you, but I don't. Can I sum up my favorite store in two words: HomeGoods? I also spend hours in the aisles of Target—especially the end caps with the clearance stickers. However, here's one quick shopping tip: Never buy anything on clearance you wouldn't pay full price for.

What one farmhouse element is a must-have?

I think every room needs a little bit of reclaimed barn wood. It's all about the imperfection and the patina. It's simple and clean with amazing detail. I've used reclaimed barn wood to make a coffee table or tray or coatracks or a dining room table. Frames are my favorite. I have some frames in my living room that are made from baseboards in our home. Barn wood is perfect for any DIY project.

What is your favorite color and why?

My favorite color is white. It's everywhere in my home. I like to wear white and design my homes with it. It's clean and bright and happy, and I've always been drawn to it. In high school, my entire shirt collection of 30 shirts were different shades of white. I still wear white, and I still decorate with it.

TOTAL INTERVIEWER ASIDE: When we went to photograph Bre's house—guess what color shirt she was wearing. White. Obvi.

How does your faith influence your design?

I love to fill my rooms with things that inspire me. Faith is such a big part of my life, and my spaces are full of subtle reminders of the gifts that God has given me. For example, in my living room, there is a distressed wood sign with Proverbs 24:3-4: "By wisdom a house is built, and through understanding it is established; through knowledge its rooms are filled with rare and beautiful treasures." This is a statement piece in our home of what I believe.

A Farmhouse Kitchen

The key to creating a farmhouse look is creating an experience with the sights and smells and textures of a sunny afternoon on the farm. Do you have a space you want to add a little farmhouse to? Here are some specific elements to add to your design to introduce a little farm to your home.

GALVANIZED METAL

Metal is found everywhere on a farm. There are feeders and pails and buckets and tools. Finding vintage farm equipment, such as antique buckets, is an easy way to add a little farmhouse charm to your décor. There are also hundreds of reproductions created from galvanized metal on the market today.

TEXTILES

Fabrics are part of everyday life on the farm. There is the soft, clean feel of flour sack, the heavier grainy texture of burlap feed sacks, and the timeless farmhouse patterns such as checks and plaids and stripes. Create a valance from vintage fabrics. Display stacks of folded dish towels in a basket, or layer grain-sack pillows on a farmhouse bench.

BREADBOARDS

One simple and easy way to add farmhouse style to the kitchen is with a collection of breadboards. You can find them at vintage shops and thrift stores and yard sales. Or you could simply DIY one of your own. Layer your collection in a plate rack, stack on a counter, or create a hanging display on the kitchen wall.

WHITE PLATTERS

Look for vintage platters with a crackled finish in places and a rich, yellowed patina. The key to displaying farmhouse platters is to add different colors of white and cream to your collection. This creates the look of a collection that has been created over time.

diy Display your platters in a DIY plate rack. To make your own, build a frame out of 1" x 2" molding pieces and attach it to the wall. Next, add in horizontal molding pieces to create shelving for the plates. Lastly, nail decorative molding pieces to the frame to hold plates in place.

HERBS

Add an organic freshness to your farmhouse kitchen with pots of fresh herbs. Grow your own herb garden in miniature galvanized pots, and DIY your own herb markers from stamped spoons or clip-on chalkboard labels. Adding a little greenery to the kitchen adds a fresh, clean look in your space.

diy Make your own herb markers for your kitchen. Flatten vintage silver plate spoons, stamp with the name of the herb, and insert into the herb pots.

FARMHOUSE STYLE DETAILS

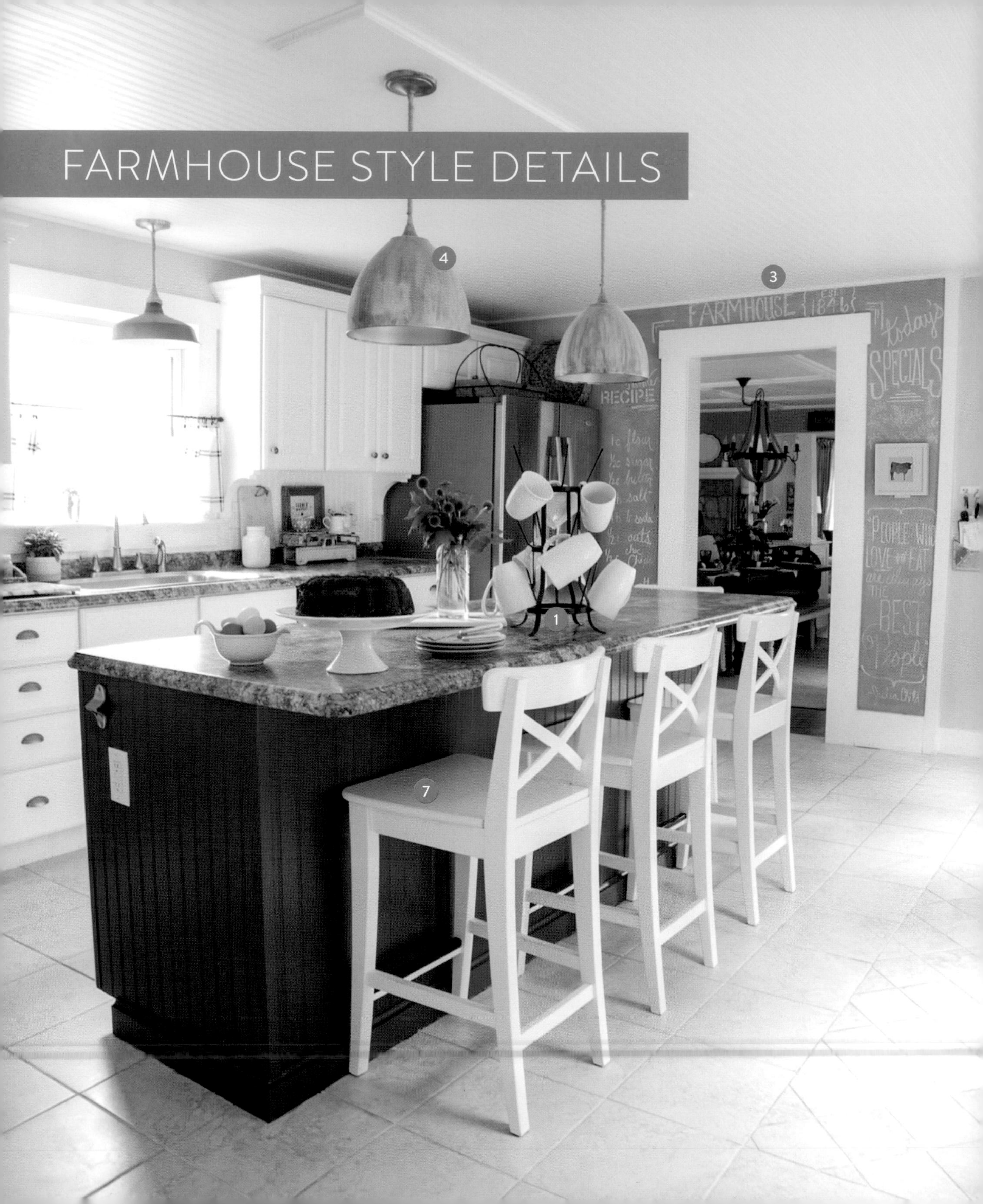

1. Create a conversation area on the kitchen island with a coffee bar.

2. Stack oversized crates for storage under a bench.

3. Add a fun design element like a chalkboard wall to the space.

4. Choose farmhouse pendant lights in a variety of colors and materials.

5. Fill a bucket with fresh greens from the yard.

6. DIY your own frames for the wall from vintage molding.

7. Add extra seating to the kitchen with bar stools and a reclaimed wood bench.

8. Simple roman shades or woven blinds bring texture to the windows.

9. Add an oversized plate rack full of yard sale dishes to the wall.

Traditional Style

When I first walked into Yvonne's kitchen, I rounded the back corner and sighed. There was an incredible display of hooks attached to plates. Each plate on each hook was a different pattern and different size. And then? Hung from each of the hooks was a patterned apron, and an oversized blue platter was hung above the hooks in the hall to complete the space.

All that pattern. All that color. All those aprons.

The most amazing thing about the display was the creative, inventive idea to take something as utilitarian as a plate—something that a traditional kitchen uses every day—and repurpose it into something else. To take a traditional style element and give it a new purpose.

That's a kitchen—traditional style. Want to add a little traditional style and repurposing to your kitchen? Here are some style tips to get you started.

ACCENT PIECES

In a traditional kitchen, select wood bar stools with a patterned or slipcovered seat. In addition, a wall of open, glass-fronted cabinets filled with a collection of plates and cups and bowls is one of the staples of traditional style. You can easily create a look like this in your own kitchen. Many cabinet doors come with a center that can be removed and replaced with glass. A local glassmaker can help. Contact one in your area to help transform your cabinets.

LIGHTING

Select a large, central, traditional fixture for over the kitchen island. Here, an oversized fixture, created to mimic a grouping of candles, brings drama and traditional design to the space. A sparkling chandelier with a drum shade or square brass cage pendants are good choices for the kitchen island as well.

HARDWARE

Choose hardware for the kitchen that's classic and timeless in design. Crystal knobs and coordinating decorative crystal handles are always a good option. Or select brass handles with a curved front with matching brass knobs. Traditional hardware is designed to complement the existing décor, adding a little jewelry to the kitchen.

COUNTERTOP DÉCOR

Sometimes the simplicity of a simple grouping of white dishes accents the countertops in style. Here, a basket filled with whiteware accentuates the depth and character of the black countertops. Coffee supplies are stored in galvanized containers next to monogrammed coffee mugs. Clear glass jars filled with nuts or snacks are lined up against the backsplash. Add a vintage teacup for easy scooping.

Transitional Style

In the middle of my kitchen is a DIY zinc magnetic memo board my brother built for me several years ago. Dozens of magnets hold things on the board. It's filled with graduation announcements and invitations and reminders and notes that make me smile. Somewhere in the middle of the jumble is a single index card with lines of hand-scrawled words to a song on it. It's my father's handwriting. He penned a verse of the song I was named after, "Kari Waits for Me," to share with my husband on the night before our wedding. It's like having a little bit of my father and my wedding and a song from the heart with me in my kitchen to help celebrate each and every day.

That's a kitchen—transitional style. Want to add a little transitional style and a note-covered memo board to your kitchen? Here are some style tips to get you started.

ACCENT PIECES

Add shelving and ledges to your transitional style kitchen to create visual interest and a place to display collections. Here, a ledge holds a set of vintage bowling pins and canisters. Select bar stools for the space with stained or painted wood and a textured seat woven from natural fibers.

diy Create an oversized clock for the space from pallet wood. Cut out a base for the clock using pallet wood and plywood. Stencil on numbers, and finish the project with a clock kit with a mechanism and hands.

LIGHTING

Lighting can be a little eclectic for the space. Mix and match elements to fit the style of your transitional space. Choose light fixtures with dramatic flair, such as this set of decorative metal pendants, or keep it simple with a patterned drum shade. Different zones of the kitchen have different lighting needs. Combine a central fixture over the kitchen island with task lighting for each of these zones.

HARDWARE

A transitional kitchen is the perfect place to go all vintage with the hardware. Search online, thrift stores, or yard sales for vintage knobs and handles. Choose antique brass knobs with a lightly patterned surface and an aged patina, and select vintage drawer pulls in a variety of shapes and textures. In a transitional kitchen, the hardware doesn't have to match. Mix it up a little in your kitchen drawers and cabinets with different patterns and styles.

COUNTERTOP DÉCOR

Place an oversized tray on the kitchen counter and accessorize it for your day. Include vintage salt and pepper shakers, a mixing bowl full of fresh fruit, and a stack of plates. Fill a crock or urn with kitchen spoons and serving pieces. Tuck a small breadboard behind a display on the counter. Even the cleaning supplies can be displayed in style. Place sponges in a jadeite bowl next to a small mason jar of fresh flowers.

Contemporary Style

I didn't see the stools at first when I entered Carmel's kitchen. I saw beautiful white cabinets, a large farmhouse sink, a black island, and creamy stone countertops. We were talking and laughing, and I was in the middle of a story about getting lost on the way to her house and ending up on an island, when all of a sudden I stopped in my tracks.

And stood speechless. Red? Bar stools?

I couldn't even with the amazing. I told Carmel how brilliant she was. Where had those stools been my whole life? They made the kitchen laugh and twirl and dance and come alive. A little pop of red pulled up to the bar in the middle of the kitchen made it sing.

And all I wanted to do was harmonize.

That's a kitchen—contemporary style. Want to add a little contemporary style and a little bit of speechless amazing to your kitchen? Here are some style tips to get you started.

ACCENT PIECES

Beyond red bar stools, there are dozens of other accent pieces to fill your contemporary kitchen. Roll in a drink cart and fill it with colorful kitschy accessories. Layer polka-dotted accessories, brilliantly patterned mugs, and a grouping of flamingo stir sticks. Even your appliances can be fun. Pour your coffee from a red coffeemaker. Mix your smoothies with a red blender. Add color to the space whenever, wherever, however you can.

> **TOTAL DECORATING ASIDE:**
> Contemporary dishes are eclectic.
> They don't really have to match.
> They just need to look like they belong.
> Kind of like stirrup pants and scrunchies.

LIGHTING

Go big or go home when it comes to contemporary lighting. Select bold, graphic lighting that makes a statement. Here, two oversized black wicker pendants hung from simple black metal rods bring drama and personality to the kitchen island. Choose a drum pendant with a black-and-white pattern for visual impact or a modern brass chandelier with crisp lines and metal detailing.

HARDWARE

Make a statement with your hardware as well. Pair sculptural drawer pulls that resemble art with simple knobs. Mix metallics in the space, combining brass with plated nickel. Choose knobs and handles made out of unusual materials, like agate slices, or add shimmer with mosaic handles created from metal and stone.

COUNTERTOP DÉCOR

Add pattern and color to the countertop with brightly colored jars filled with kitchen spoons and serving pieces. Create a fun display with a variety of patterned coffee mugs. Group bowls of fruit on a tray with fresh flowers. Display a vintage Lucite tray with a bold, graphic pattern on the countertop for a pop of graphic color.

diy Make your own art for the kitchen countertop with a clipboard. Find a piece of colorful art that works with your design. Clip it onto a vintage clipboard, and display on your kitchen counters.

Coastal Style

When my great-grandfather was dating my great-grandmother, he drove her in a sleigh out to the location where our beach house is built now. They envisioned the community and the getaway for their family, and together they planned a life for future generations. Eventually, they got married and built their first house together. The table that sits in our beach house next to the kitchen came from my great-grandparents' house. It could write a bestselling novel featuring the stories of generations of family gatherings. The drama. The laughter. The milestones—all celebrated around the kitchen table.

That's a kitchen—coastal style. Want to add a little coastal and some chapters in a bestselling novel to your kitchen? Here are some style tips to get you started.

ACCENT PIECES

One simple way to add coastal style to a kitchen is with small accent pieces. Pull up brightly colored bar stools to the counter. Tuck a chair in a corner for simple kitchen conversation during meal planning. Add a drink cart with drinks and mugs and mixes for late-night hot chocolate or afternoon sweet tea.

diy Transform a bar stool with a fresh coat of paint in fire engine red or sunshine yellow or brilliant black, and then hand-letter or stencil a quote or scripture.

LIGHTING

Keep lighting simple in your coastal style décor with lighted ceiling fans. Bring the ocean breezes into your space with fans that help circulate the air. Choose a ceiling fan with wood blades or even a natural fiber like bamboo for over the kitchen table. Looking for a statement lighting fixture instead of a ceiling fan for your kitchen? Why not select an oyster shell or capiz shell pendant for over the kitchen island?

HARDWARE

Doorknobs and handles are an easy place to add a little fun to your kitchen. Add color to your kitchen cabinets with brightly colored glass knobs and hardware. Create a coastal style kitchen with starfish and sea horse handles and knobs.

 Make your own hardware with simple pieces of rope threaded through holes in the cabinet drawers and then knotted in the back to stay in place.

TOTAL DECORATING ASIDE:
Cookbooks make great accent pieces in a kitchen. I know. I don't cook with my cookbooks. I just decorate with them.

COUNTERTOP DÉCOR

Coastal style for your countertops can be as simple as a stack of cookbooks topped with a shell found on a recent beach excursion. Fill a clear, aqua-colored glass vase with oyster shells and with a bunch of fresh flowers from the yard. Or create a vignette with a grouping of white vases with a DIY jute twine and seashell garland draped around them.

 String shells and sand dollars on jute twine, spacing them about 4 inches apart. Use the garland to decorate the mantel, bookcases, or to drape over a centerpiece.

TRANSITIONAL

Every kitchen needs a space to show off—a place to display what makes it special and unique. Enter the kitchen hutch. Sometimes it's ornate and full of character—a piece handed down from generation to generation. Sometimes it's simply a painted yard sale piece.

This black hutch is full of heirlooms and unique pieces. A collection of white dishes creates a contrast with the patina of the hutch. Hand-painted tole trays bring color and vintage charm to the display.

FARMHOUSE

Decorate a farmhouse hutch with a collection of dishes from whiteware plates and platters to the rich patina of vintage silver plate. Include glass vases, breadboards, pitchers and creamers, baskets, vintage signs, and cloches.

CONTEMPORARY

Bold and graphic with clean lines, this contemporary hutch adds drama and personality to the space. A collection of colorful, patterned dishes takes center stage next to an oversized mirror.

TRADITIONAL

This traditional hutch is filled with layers of the owner's collection of white dishes. Vases and jars are filled with a collection of vintage silver plate, and these tiny, painted, vintage egg cups create a whimsical, timeless feel.

COASTAL

The key to adding coastal style to a hutch is keeping it simple. Start by painting the back of the hutch a dark navy and then layer in fresh flowers from the yard. Here milk glass and hydrangeas create a cool, breezy feeling.

Wood
Slice Tray

SKILL LEVEL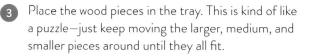

Supplies

4 packages
birch wood slices
(approximately 60 total slices)

wood tray

wood glue

acrylic sealer

Instructions

 Open the packages and separate the wood slices into larger pieces, medium pieces, and smaller pieces.

2 Remove excess bark from the edges of the wood pieces.

3 Place the wood pieces in the tray. This is kind of like a puzzle—just keep moving the larger, medium, and smaller pieces around until they all fit.

4 After you have your pattern established, place a small dot of wood glue on the back of the wood slices and glue in place.

 Let dry.

 Seal the top of the wood slices with acrylic sealer.

The Bathroom

5

The Room That
Takes On the Day

In my new (old) house, there's a bathroom with a mirror that has chronicled my life. It cheered at the sight of the oversized mum I wore to Friday night football games. It rolled its eyes at the navy-blue sweater vest with the plaid bows I wore on my first date with my husband. It smiled the day I stood with my Aqua Net coiffure, bright red lipstick, and black liquid eyeliner in a wedding dress with yards and yards of beaded satin and a monogrammed train. The mirror never missed a day.

The afternoon my mother sold the house, I paused one final time to look in that mirror. The eyes that stared back at me were so sad. It was the end of an era. I left the bathroom and the mirror and reached for the handle of the back door when suddenly—I stopped.

I couldn't help it. Walking back into the bathroom, I reached up with both hands. And ran out the back door with the mirror.

It came home with me and I tucked it away for five years. *Until.* Until the day we bought back the house from the couple my mother had sold it to. With a happy heart, I carried in the mirror and hung it up in the bathroom. Right where it belonged. Right back home.

That's the thing about bathrooms. They might be decorated with different styles, but in the end, the bathroom is always there. It's the room that shines and spiffs you up and sends you out to take on the day.

Let's take a look at a variety of bathrooms decorated in different styles with a few organizing tips along the way.

Traditional Style

Most of us think of traditional style when we think of bathrooms. All the things in all the right places. Stacks of fresh towels. Hand soap that smells like lavender. Oversized mirrors in carved frames. A vase of fresh flowers. A vintage chair. A sparkling chandelier. All of these elements work together to define traditional bathroom style.

Simple. Classic. Timeless.

Ready to add a little tradition to your bathroom? Looking for inspiration and ideas? Here are some specific elements that introduce traditional style to your space.

WHITE TILE

Create a traditional look with white tile in a bathroom. White tile is classic and timeless, but it doesn't have to be boring. Combine tiles in a variety of shapes and sizes and patterns to mix it up a little. Lay tiles on the diagonal or in a traditional subway, herringbone, chevron, or basket weave pattern. Add a twist to traditional white tile with colored grout. Choose a dark gray or taupe grout to add visual interest and make the tile pattern pop. One added bonus? Darker grout hides the dirt.

MONOGRAMMED LINENS

Nothing says traditional bathroom style like monogrammed linens. Order a set of monogrammed towels online and stack them on a stool next to the shower or tub. You can also find vintage monogrammed linens at thrift stores. The softness of vintage linens makes them the perfect accessory in a bathroom. Fold and place next to the sink for guests.

CLASSIC FURNITURE

Every traditional bathroom needs a piece of classic furniture. Here, a white chair with classic lines is pulled up to the counter of this traditional bathroom. A chair or stool is also the perfect place to add a stitched monogrammed pillow or handwoven basket of favorite magazines or books to the space.

VINTAGE ARTWORK

Decorate the walls of a traditional bathroom with vintage artwork. Botanical prints in gold frames or tiny prints framed in wood bring an element of classic design to the space. Shop for vintage artwork at local flea markets, and find pieces that make your space happy. It's one of the easiest ways to add a little color and personality to your room.

diy If you don't have a collection of art pieces, here's a simple DIY. Frame pages of a vintage book instead. Remove colorful prints or drawings from the book, cut to size, and frame for personalized art for the wall.

FRAMED MIRRORS

One way to add traditional style to your bathroom is with an oversized mirror. Rather than a wall of mirror, opt for framed mirrors instead. Here, a large, ornate mirror anchors the space, and the carved frame creates a contrast with the clean lines of the tile.

tip Search for the perfect empty frame at yard sales or thrift stores, and bring it to a local glassmaker to create your own unique mirror for a lot less.

Farmhouse Style

I watched Bre's farmhouse bathroom transformation on her blog. It was cute before. It had gray and white stripes with painted baskets and a clean, airy feel. *How in the world can she make it cuter?* I thought. *Is it even possible?*

And then? I saw the finished room and my mouth dropped open. The transformation was incredible and amazing and awe inspiring.

This "after" stole my heart.

That's the amazing thing about farmhouse style. It changes with the seasons. One minute it's light and airy and smells like lavender-scented sheets hanging on the line. Then, in a blink of an eye, it evolves and embraces warm, rich colors and dark metals and pops of color.

Ready to add a little farmhouse to your bathroom? Here are some specific elements that introduce farmhouse style to your space.

INDUSTRIAL LIGHT FIXTURES

One of the simplest places to add a little farmhouse to your space is by adding a little industrial style with your lighting selections. Choose a galvanized metal fixture with simple lines and industrial elements for over the sink. Add a pendant fixture with a pulley system and simple cage light to the center of the bathroom ceiling. Finish off all your lighting fixtures with classic Edison bulbs found in most big box home improvement stores.

FRESH FLOWERS

Keep your flowers simple and sweet in a farmhouse bathroom. Collect daisies and add them to a glass milk pitcher on the bathroom counter. Add a bunch of fresh greenery cut from the yard to a vintage glass bottle. Place tiny potted plants in the window, or DIY your own topiary from a potted English ivy for the bathroom shelf.

WOOD ELEMENTS

Reclaimed wood décor adds a fresh, organic feel to a space. Place a wood tray on top of a small hutch or bookcase and add small containers for brushes and other bathroom necessities. Here, a botanical print framed with wood pieces and hung with jute twine creates a unique piece of farmhouse artwork.

COLOR

Farmhouse style has a variety of color palettes. For example, gray ticking and airy sheers and bright, white cotton linens create a clean, crisp, neutral color palette. Amp up the drama with a darker version of the neutral theme with dark gray walls, vintage brass accents, and painted furniture in rich, vivid colors.

VINTAGE FURNITURE

Add a little farmhouse style with a piece of vintage furniture in the bathroom. Repurpose a vintage piece as a vanity by cutting a hole in the top of a dresser or sideboard and adding a drop-in sink.

Finish the look with a vintage faucet. Vintage reproduction faucets come in a variety of styles including porcelain handles and antique finishes.

Transitional Style

I have never painted a bathroom purple before. Not because I have anything against purple. I like the smell of lavender. I like violets and grapes and sea urchins and peacock feathers and a hint of purple in my sunsets. I'd just never envisioned it for a bathroom before until I saw Laura's space. A light, quiet purple with just the right amount of dusky.

The brilliant thing about the purple is that it allowed the vintage pieces of Laura's transitional style bathroom to shine. All because of a little purple.

Ready to add a little transitional style to your bathroom? Here are some specific elements that introduce transitional style to your space.

A BIT OF WHIMSY

Transitional style is all about the creative and the unique. Repurpose and reuse vintage accessories to decorate your space. Frame family quotes or scriptures in handmade yardstick frames for an easy, personalized piece of wall art.

diy Add whimsy by turning a faucet handle into a tassel. Tie bits of ribbons and burlap to the spokes of the faucet, wrap jute twine around the center, and hang on a doorknob in the bathroom.

METALLIC ACCENTS

Create depth and visual interest in a space with metallic accents. Every room looks better with a little sparkle. Include metal baskets for organizing, galvanized buckets to hold accessories, and vintage metal containers to hold fresh flowers. In a transitional space, metals don't have to match. Create an eclectic look with different styles and finishes.

ECLECTIC LIGHT FIXTURES

A transitional style is all about mixing and matching, and light fixtures are no exception. In Laura's transitional bathroom, a sparkling chandelier adds twinkling light to the space. Try a wooden bead chandelier or a metal floral light fixture. Choose what you love, and it will work in the space.

CRATES

Baskets and crates are a great way to add extra storage to the bathroom. Create an organizer for your bathroom with vintage coffee crates. Start with a small crate and attach casters to the bottom. The casters allow the crate to move from one side of the bathroom to the other as needed.

diy Make a bath caddy. Take a 10" x 4' pine board. Next, attach two pieces of 1" x 1" x 4" pine board to the back, approximately 4 inches in from each side. Attach handles to each end of the pine board.

RECLAIMED WOOD

There's something about wood with a history. The lines and the patina and the stories its grains can tell. Introduce history into the bathroom with the character of reclaimed wood. Accessorize the space with wood frames, signs, and trays.

Contemporary Style

When I went to decorate my first official bathroom, I was all about the black and white.

I'd pore over decorating magazines, and I had files of magazine clippings. I painted the walls khaki and found black-and-white accessories for everything. But the crowning glory of the bathroom? The one thing that made it stand up and be counted?

The striped black-and-white shower curtain with tiny hotel shower clips.

Now my bathrooms are farmhouse. But when I walked into Carmel's bathroom and saw her light fixtures with the tiny striped black-and-white shades? They made my heart beat faster and sigh for all the shower curtains that have gone before.

Ready to add a little contemporary to your bathroom? Here are some specific elements that introduce contemporary style to your space.

PATTERN

A contemporary bathroom is full of bold patterns and graphic design elements. Stripes and polka dots and geometric prints layered against a white background work together to bring a crisp, clean, colorful style to the space. Wallpaper a wall in a brilliant print. Add in fabrics with an overall graphic design. Or paint a single piece of furniture in a bold pattern. The key is to select one design element and then create a bold statement.

POPS OF COLOR

Just as with pattern, go big and bold with colors for the bath. Carmel painted her vanity a brilliant shade of pink. The sink, combined with the white subway tile and the wood flooring, truly brings the space to life. The same vivid choice of color is repeated on the hand towels on the ladder, adding in a fresh, green botanical print as well.

BOLD ART PRINTS

Make a statement with your art in a contemporary bathroom. Order prints from contemporary artists and frame them in simple metallic or white frames. Choose bold, graphic pieces that make you smile. Don't take your art or your bathroom too seriously. Have fun and choose what speaks to you.

diy Use an online graphics program to design an art piece for your space around a simple repeated design. For example, take a lemon and repeat it over and over again for dramatic effect.

TEXTURE

This contemporary bathroom is full of texture. The subway tile is juxtaposed against a vintage ladder doubling as a towel rack. The smooth texture of the pink sink contrasts with the depth and movement of the planks on the wood floor. Stack baskets with

colorful towels, add in vintage rugs, and choose wood slice bath organizers for additional texture. Choose plants with sculptural appeal for texture, such as a cactus or grouping of succulents. Add plants to simple terra-cotta pots or silver or brass planters. Add additional texture by creating your own planter out of cording and macramé knots.

Coastal Style

I come from a long line of creative bathroom decorators. My grandmother wallpapered the walls of our beach house with comic strips—a little light reading when you washed your face? Thinking about it still makes me laugh.

And then?

One day my mother decided the comic strips had to go. It was the end of an era. The room now is airy and white with beadboard and pom-pom curtains. I miss those comics, but even though they are gone, one thing remains the same. You can still hear the sound of the waves crashing onto the shore just outside the window.

Ready to add a little coastal to your bathroom? Here are some specific elements that introduce coastal style to your space.

LIGHT AND AIRY

Decorating a coastal bathroom is all about bringing the feel of ocean inside. Choose fabrics and textiles that have movement and light. For example, sheers at the window bring in light and provide privacy at the same time. Stacks of clean white towels on a train rack organizer create a crisp, clean feeling. Keep the walls and trim light and bright.

tip Painting the trim in a high gloss sheen reflects light and creates a durable finish for a challenging coastal climate.

ORGANIC ELEMENTS

Coastal style is all about bringing the outside in. Shop the beach for creative décor ideas for your rooms. Tie starfish or sand dollars onto the shower curtain hooks for a little coastal flair, or paint one of your favorite quotes onto a rock as a doorstop. Add fresh flowers to your space with a few creative containers. Cover a glass vase in twigs from the beach for a unique idea. Or use colorful sea glass or pebbles from the beach to anchor flowers in a glass vase.

diy Find a long piece of driftwood and attach ready-made hooks from the hardware store to the wood. Hang on the wall and use to organize towels and beach accessories.

COLOR

Start with a calm, neutral palette for your coastal bathroom. Different shades of white and cream create an airy, beachy feel to your space. You can also add a little color to your space with accessories in a color such as navy or turquoise. Here, a piece of string anchor art adds color to this brilliantly white bathroom.

diy At the craft store, look for beach-themed, unfinished wood cutouts, paint them navy or turquoise. Glue to a piece of reclaimed wood to create your very own piece of beach art.

VINTAGE PIECES

One of my favorite things to do when I spend the summer at the beach is shop the local thrift stores. Adding a little vintage to any space creates authenticity and a bit of whimsy. Here, a vintage locker basket is stacked on a vintage stool and filled with crisp, fresh linens for the bathroom. Look for vintage hardware, hooks, or buttons to repurpose in your coastal bathroom.

Stylish Bathroom Organization

When it comes to bathrooms, I am asked one question over and over again: How do I add more storage to my bathroom? In most bathrooms, space is limited. There is a lot of stuff to store in a bathroom and not a lot of space to store it in. Looking for bathroom organizational ideas? Here are some of my favorites:

REPURPOSED TOOLBOX—Recycle a toolbox into a towel holder. Turn the toolbox on its side, hang on the wall with the handle out. The toolbox transforms into a shelf to organize bathroom necessities, and the handle becomes a towel holder.

LADDER—Place a ladder against one wall and use as a bathroom organizer. Layer on fresh towels and hand towels for easy guest access.

SHELLS—In a coastal bathroom, shells make instant organizers. Pick up some large shells on your next trip to the beach. Clean, bleach, and lay out in the sun to dry. Then use to organize Q-tips, cotton balls, rings, and other small bathroom items.

PEG HOOKS—Have a large family? Instead of a towel bar, maximize space with long peg hooks. Hang boards with peg hooks end to end, allowing room for up to ten towels and hand towels instead of one or two.

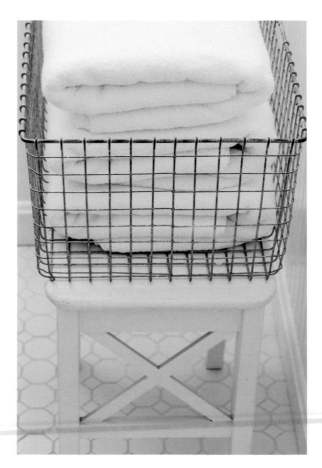

VINTAGE LOCKER BASKETS—Recycle locker baskets in the bathroom. Place a locker basket on top of a stool. Fill with stacked towels, magazines, extra shampoo and conditioner, or washcloths.

REPURPOSE—Think outside the box when it comes to bathroom organization. Hang a vintage washboard on the wall. Tie a string on each side and knot in place. Add wood clothespins, and clip a linen hand towel into place.

FLIP THE SCRIPT—Get creative with your shelving. Take a standard wall shelf held up by brackets and flip it over so the brackets are on top. The brackets help keep bathroom items in place and create visual interest in a small space.

THE DOORS HAVE IT—If you have enough wall space on the exterior of a bathroom, hang a sliding barn door to maximize wall space inside the room. Pocket doors that slide away into the wall are also a great option for a bathroom door.

BE LAZY—A lazy Susan can be your best friend. Place one underneath the sink and fill it with bathroom necessities. Then, to access, simply spin around until you find exactly what you were looking for.

THE FORGOTTEN SPACE—Don't forget the cabinet doors. Add small baskets or a row of hooks just inside the cabinet doors. Use to organize hair accessories and styling products.

EXTRA STORAGE—You can find a little storage where you least expect it. Right behind door number one. Purchase over-the-door hooks and place on top of the door. Use to hang extra towels, robes, or other items.

UPCYCLE—Repurpose an old drawer from a previous DIY project into a bathroom organizer. Hang the drawer vertically on the wall. Add hooks on the inside of the drawer. Use to organize your necklaces and other jewelry.

The Bedroom

6

Dream a Little Dream

I grew up in a time when all things matched.

You know.

The wallpaper matched the bedding, which matched the dust ruffle, which matched the shams. My bedroom growing up was a Laura Ashley bedroom, and the entire room was full of pattern. The walls were a dusky blue background with a tiny cream all-over print. The bedding was a reverse of the same pattern with matching fluffy pillowcases and a bed skirt that ruffled its way into two counties.

At the risk of stating the obvious, it was amazing.

My room was my castle. I spent many a lazy afternoon ensconced in a stuffed chair in the corner dreaming. Dreaming of what I would be when I grew up and my future self and what I wanted to do and be and wondering if there was a life beyond my four Laura Ashley wallpapered walls.

And now?

One of my twin daughters lives in that same bedroom. When we moved back to the house I grew up in, she chose that room for herself. It looks a little different now. The walls aren't Laura Ashley anymore. The wallpaper has long ago left the building. Now the walls are painted white shiplap decorated with calligraphied wood signs, a gold ampersand, a gallery wall full of pictures, and an oversized round mirror. The bed is an antique four-poster with gold polka-dotted sheets, matching shams, furry pillows, and a white down comforter.

But the dreaming?

It's still the same. Because that's what bedrooms are for. Hoping and dreaming and planning and imagining the future. A respite from the world. A safe haven. A warm and welcoming retreat. A place where we can kick off our shoes, surround ourselves with comfort, sink into furry pillows, and leave our cares behind.

Before we take a look at different bedrooms from the perspective of each design style, let's begin with a few principles of bedroom design. If a bedroom makeover is in your future, here are a few simple tips to get you started.

Layer in Cozy

When designing the space, take into account that the primary focus of the bedroom is to create a retreat. Amp up the cozy. Start with the bedding. Choose fluffy down comforters with crisp, cotton duvet covers. Make sure the sheets are soft and made of natural fibers to allow the linens to breathe. Add several down throw pillows to the bed to layer in comfort. Tuck an upholstered chair into a corner, and add a throw to the chair to make sure the space has extra coziness.

Lighting

When choosing lighting for a bedroom, make sure to add different sources of lighting for different tasks. For example, place two table lamps, one on either side of the bed, for bedside lighting. Don't have room for side tables? Look into adding extendable wall sconces for either side of the bed. Add a floor lamp beside a chair in the bedroom for extra light when reading. Choose an overhead fixture or can light for the room to provide enough overall light for the bedroom.

Ceiling Fan

The question I get asked the most about bedroom decorating? To ceiling fan or to not ceiling fan. The answer is completely dependent on the individual. Some people need ceiling fans in a bedroom for air circulation, especially in the South. Fortunately, amazing new designs for ceiling fan designs are on the market. Add farmhouse style with a cage light and warm wooden blades. Looking for a contemporary fixture? Select a sleek brass design with clean lines and additional blades. There is a ceiling fan for every design style. Whether you choose to decorate with one is up to you.

Texture

Neutral bedding and bedrooms are trending right now. No matter the design style or aesthetic, more and more bedrooms are turning up neutral. If a neutral bedroom is in your future, it doesn't have to be boring. Let the room shine by adding in texture to the space. Start with your textiles. Thick cotton fabrics with a heavy weave or crisp linens with monograms are perfect for adding drama to a neutral space. Bring in additional texture with woven baskets, natural fiber rugs, and woven throws tossed over the end of the bed.

Music

One of the simplest ways to create a spa-like retreat in the bedroom is with music. Gone are the days of expensive speakers and elaborate music systems. Creating atmosphere with music is as simple as reaching for your phone. You can purchase a small tabletop speaker to connect to your phone via Bluetooth or create your own for the bedroom. Then choose the playlist that fits your mood, sit back, and relax in your retreat.

Contemporary Style
Q & A with Carmel

It was a rainy day when we turned down the road to Carmel's house. A summer storm was blowing in off the coast and sweeping raindrops across the roads as we drove down the winding streets of the neighborhood. "You'll know it's my house when you see the door," Carmel had told me with a laugh when she gave me directions. Pausing to check that I was on the right street, I searched the passing house numbers for the correct address. *And then?* I saw it. Carmel's front door standing out from the crowd.

Painted pink.

It was amazing. In the middle of all the blacks and grays and neutrals, that front door danced in the rain. That's the thing about contemporary style. It stands out in a crowd. It takes names and shows up and represents and gets noticed. It's bold and colorful and celebrates the joy of a pink door surrounded by gray skies and raindrops.

Carmel lives in Charleston, South Carolina, with her husband, two children, and her two schnauzers, Gandalph and Elsa. Carmel enjoys reading, thrifting, long walks on the beach, and binge-watching Netflix shows. She loves living close to the ocean, and she brings home a shell from every trip. Her house is full of color and timeless, eclectic pieces she has collected over the years. Interesting Carmel fact: She wasn't really all about decorating when she was younger, but now? Her heart is to truly create a beautiful setting for herself and her family.

What one contemporary item is a must-have for a space?

No matter what house I've lived in, I've always been drawn to a one-of-a-kind rug. My favorite rug is my vintage red rug in the living room. It was such a bargain. I got it for only $50 from a local antique booth that was going out of business. My other go-to design items are mirrors. We have an incredible mirror in our dining room. It's made up of three different pieces that hang over my sideboard and reflect the light from across the room. It feels like a piece of art that's a mirror.

Do you have any designers who inspire you?

I'm so glad that *Trading Spaces* is back on television. Laurie Smith is one of my favorites. She truly inspires me. Genevieve Gorder is another *Trading Spaces* alum I follow. I like the way she weaves organic pieces and natural textures into a space. Also, Miles Redd is amazing. He's so bold with his color choices, and I've pinned a million of his images.

What is your favorite color and why?

My favorite color is red. When I was growing up, I had a red Radio Flyer tricycle with silver streamers on the handlebars. I remember pedaling it all around and living my best life. From there, red just stuck with me. I love red lipstick, and I wear red shoes and red pants. My first car was red. I wore a red dress to prom. Red has been with me my whole life, and it's never failed me yet.

What design books are on your bookshelf?

Novel Interiors by Lisa Borgness Giramonti. I read it years ago, and it's still on my bookshelf today. The cover of the book is a red room—red walls with a red sofa with a red carpet. As you look through the pages of the book, one thing stands out—the rooms look lived in. Nothing is perfect. Nothing is overly styled. It's like taking a tour of a house that is well loved and getting to see all the behind the scenes. That concept inspired my own design philosophy.

What is one piece of advice you would give to someone about decorating?

My best piece of advice would be to go with what you love. There are so many different decorating styles out there right now. It's easy to lose sight of what you like with all the photographs and ideas on blogs and magazines and television shows. Don't re-create something just because someone else has it in their home. Choose what speaks to you, and decorate from the heart.

A Contemporary Bedroom

Do you have a bedroom in which you want to amp up the style? Here are some specific elements to add to your spaces that introduce your room to contemporary style.

COLOR

This style isn't just about adding color. It's about adding color in the right way. Choose where you want to go bold with your color and make a statement. For example, select one piece of furniture in the space and paint it a vibrant, vivid color, such as canary yellow or fire engine red or eggplant purple. Then select a few other key pieces to add additional color, and keep the rest of the room neutral. The key is to choose bold color and make it count.

BOLD FABRICS

Just as with color, you want your fabrics to make a statement. Layer bold black stripes with a larger overall floral or oversized buffalo check. Use the 60-30-10 rule when choosing fabric for your space. Select the graphic pattern you want to make the most impact, and use it 60 percent of the time. Next, choose a complementary pattern, and use it in 30 percent of your decorating. Lastly, add a final complementary pattern, and layer it into the space 10 percent of the time.

WHIMSICAL ART

Make a statement on your walls with art. Choose art that sparks conversation—art that is bold and colorful or whimsical with a story. The key is to add art to the space that draws the eye and speaks to your unique perspective. The contemporary space is full of one-of-a-kind pieces, and art should be no exception.

DARK CEILINGS

When choosing the paint palette for the space, look up. Select a dark, moody gray or dark navy for the ceiling to add drama. Keep the rest of the walls neutral, and allow the ceiling to shine. Another fun tip to draw the eye upward is to paint a pattern on the ceiling or make a bold statement with a ceiling medallion.

ACRYLIC FURNITURE

Furniture for a contemporary space should be creative and unique. Add an acrylic chair to a desk. The shine and patina of the chair bring clean lines and a contemporary perspective to the room. Make the chair stand out even more with a fun, graphic pillow in a vivid color or geometric pattern.

CONTEMPORARY STYLE DETAILS

 Add drama to a space with a large, central light fixture like this woven pendant.

 Go bold with an azure blue rug to add a contrasting color to the space.

 Paint the ceiling a dark, moody gray and keep the walls light and airy.

 Choose an oversized buffalo check pattern or other graphic textile for the end of the bed.

 Provide lighting for reading with a contemporary floor lamp.

 Keep curtains simple and uncluttered with clean lines and metal rods.

 Add an acrylic chair or other one-of-a-kind furniture to the space.

 Choose one furniture element to add bold color, like this brilliant red bed.

 Add graphic art and contemporary paintings to the wall to add color to the space.

Traditional Style

I still remember the first day I fell in love with tufting.

Every Christmas, our town hosts a Holiday House Tour. It takes place in the historic part of town, with tree-lined streets and wraparound porches and tiny turreted roofs and doors with their very own monograms. We never miss it.

Each year, I walk through the houses and sigh and decide this is exactly what I want my house to look like when it grows up. One year, the most amazing house I've ever seen was on the tour. It was full of vintage antiques and one-of-a-kind pieces and brilliantly shiny floors and a kitchen with hand-painted tile. I walked through the halls of the house taking in every detail. As I turned a corner off the bedroom, suddenly, there it was.

A gingham checked chair with 38 tiny tufted buttons.

One day, when my house graduates from college, I'll celebrate with tufting my chairs. That's traditional style—all the details and antique pieces and timeless style that make you sigh and sign your house up for continuing education. Want to add a little traditional and a little gingham check to your bedroom? Here are some style tips to get you started.

LINENS

A traditional bedroom is all about luxury, and linens are no exception. Add embroidered duvet covers with luxurious, high-thread-count sheets, with tailored detailing such as piping and pressed pleats. Another suggestion for a traditional bedroom is a velvet coverlet or stonewashed Belgian linen

 Mix high-end bedding with more inexpensive, timeless pieces to create the look for less.

SIDE TABLES

Go-tos for side tables in a traditional space are vintage antiques. Choose pieces with a brilliant patina and intricate details to bring character and timelessness to the space. Antique sideboards, small drop-leaf tables, vintage dressers, and a set of antique nesting tables all work well in a traditional bedroom. Mix it up a little with pieces handcrafted from different woods and stains to layer personality into the room.

LAMPS AND SHADES

Add a little personality into the space with a brilliantly patterned lamp shade. Choose a traditional base in an antique brass or mercury glass, and then add a shade in a floral damask or two-toned stripe or overall toile. Top it all off with a unique finial. Look for vintage finials at antique shops or estate sales that instantly transform the lamp into a unique piece for the space.

STORAGE

Vintage trunks with brass details or cedar boxes are ideal storage options for a traditional bedroom. Small dressers for a closet or side table are perfect storage for out-of-season clothing, extra writing supplies, or extra blankets for the bedroom. Keep blankets or linens fresh with a DIY lavender sachet.

diy Make your own sachet by stitching up the sides and adding a small hem to the top of a vintage handkerchief. Fill with dried lavender, thread a ribbon through the hem, and pull closed.

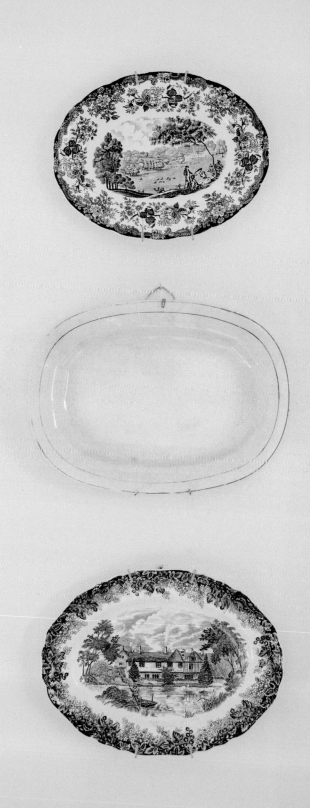

Farmhouse Style

You never know what you'll find when you shop at the side of the road.

Several years ago, in the middle of one of my brief stints at jogging, I ran right up to the most amazing thing parked at the curb. It was a bed. And not just any bed—a vintage bed with four posters and beautiful lines and carved finial feet. I stopped midjog and stared at it. Were they throwing this away? Was this piece of chippy amazingness headed for the trash pile? I knocked on the door and asked if I could have it. The owners told me it was mine if I could beat the trash truck to it.

My jogging shoes and I never ran faster in our entire lives.

I brought it home and washed off the dirt and sanded down the pieces that had gone astray and painted it gray and lightly distressed it. It now sits in an upstairs bedroom tucked away under the eaves and several layers of down comforters and a soft linen duvet cover. A little trash turned into treasure.

That's a bedroom—farmhouse style. Want to add a little farmhouse and a little trash-turned-into-treasure to your bedroom? Here are some style tips to get you started.

LINENS

One of the hallmarks of a farmhouse bedroom is the bedding itself. Light and airy, the bedding typically starts with a crisp white duvet cover or a quilt with blue ticking. Next, layers of pillows and shams—made from quilted fabrics, gingham checks, monogrammed vintage linen, or tiny calico prints—are added to the top of the bed. The bed skirt is full, with extra ruffles draping the floor. Throw pillows in the room are made from soft linen, crisp cotton ticking, and striped grain-sack fabric.

> **TOTAL DECORATING ASIDE:**
> Pallets are your best friend.
> Use them to make art, chalkboards,
> or a bench for the end of the bed.

SIDE TABLES

In a farmhouse bedroom, side tables get creative. Stack baskets or crates next to the bed to create a side table with texture and storage. Look for vintage steamer trunks or leather suitcases to use as a side table. An oversized crate or even a painted wood stump are other creative options as well.

diy Update a side table with a painted monogram top. Use carbon paper to trace your monogram on the tabletop, and then fill in the letters with paint. Lightly distress and add a finish coat to seal the monogram.

LAMPS AND SHADES

When it comes to table lamps in a farmhouse bedroom, the chunkier the better. Choose lamps with a carved silhouette in natural wood, painted white wood, or even a mercury glass finish to add a little sparkle. Keep lampshades light and airy. Select a linen, burlap, or lightly patterned white shade. Farmhouse shades also feature fun details such as buttons, pleating, ruffles, or shirred fabric.

STORAGE

Looking for storage in a farmhouse bedroom? Look no further than the end of the bed. Place a vintage bench there, and tuck wooden boxes or crates underneath to hold extra pillows or linens. Add a stack of toolboxes against one wall for extra storage for games and craft supplies. Lastly, don't forget about under the bed. Add a long, flat basket or crate on wheels for the perfect hideaway for extra comforters and blankets.

Transitional Style

Once upon a time, I decided I was going to be a needlepointist.

To this day, I'm not really sure why. I think I saw a needlepoint pillow on the pages of a glossy magazine, and I was hooked. The pillow was tucked into a chair in the corner of a bedroom, and it looked timeworn and full of character and the richness of a long-ago era. So I went to a needlepoint store and got a little bit of needlepoint instruction and bought a needlepoint kit to make a pillow and started on my needlepointing journey. First one stitch and then another and another. I spent hours threading the needle and pulling it through the canvas and trying to stay in the lines of the painted design.

Four hours later I had two rows.

My needlepoint journey slowed to a crawl. I never finished the pillow. It was too daunting of a task. Instead, I needlepointed a coaster and sewed it to the front of a pillow that I tucked into a chair in the corner of my bedroom.

A testament to the beginning and ending of my stitching career.

Just like my pillow, every transitional bedroom needs a little history, whether it's needlepoint or artwork or a family heirloom. Want to add a little transitional style and a coaster pillow to your bedroom? Here are some style tips to get you started.

LINENS

In a transitional bedroom, linens don't necessarily have to match. A bedding set with a mix of eclectic pieces creates a warm, cozy atmosphere in the space. Make your own one-of-a-kind bedding with family pieces transformed into pillows, shams, or throws. Take an old quilt that's ripped and damaged beyond repair and sew bolster pillows from it. Sew shams out of your grandmother's aprons. Or create a patchwork throw for the end of the bed from vintage linens hand-stitched together.

SIDE TABLES

Selecting furniture for the transitional space is a little like attending a wedding. There's something old, something new, something borrowed, and something blue. It's a mix of history and yard sale and your grandmother's attic. Look for functional pieces that can do double duty in a space. For example, a vintage heirloom desk makes a great side table and provides storage and space to work at as well.

LAMPS AND SHADES

When choosing table lamps for a transitional space, look for a lamp you love. Transitional is all about mixing in other styles and working with what you have. Shop your home. The perfect lamp may be just a living room away. Select the lamp shade that helps to create the mood you want for a space. Feeling dark and moody and mysterious? Choose a dark shade to filter light. Want a bright, airy space? A lamp shade in a light neutral, such as khaki or taupe, will give you the light you are looking for.

STORAGE

Add storage to a transitional space by repurposing unusual pieces. For example, transform an old apple crate into a hair accessory organizer. Use a printer's tray to organize earrings. Stack crates in the closet to organize extra shoes and purses. Cut a vintage suitcase in half and create wall shelves. Create shoe organizers from leftover pieces of molding. Simply attach to the wall and hang shoes by their heels.

Coastal Style

All those summers. All those road trips. All those long winding miles that ended at Cape Cod. We'd spend long, lazy summer days exploring the beach and having picnics on the jetties and walking across the sand looking for sea glass as the waves lapped at our feet.

On one of those trips to the beach, I found a conch shell. I'm not sure how it drifted up onto our beach. We mostly had rocks and crab legs and clamshells and periwinkles. But there it was—the most beautiful shell I'd ever seen. When I held it up to my ear and listened, I could hear the roar of the ocean waves.

A little bit of ocean I could carry home with me.

That's what a coastal bedroom feels like. A little bit of the ocean you bring home. Want to add a little coastal and a little of the sea and the sand and the tide to your bedroom? Here are some style tips to get you started.

LINENS

When creating a coastal bedroom, start with blue and white. It's timeless and coastal and brings a little of the outside in. Set off a crisp white duvet cover with layers of blue-and-white patterned blankets at the end of the bed. Choose polka dots or stripes or whimsical beach prints of starfish or sand dollars for the textiles for the space. Then layer throw pillows, curtains, and shams in coordinating patterns. If blue and white isn't your thing, there are dozens of other coastal color palettes. Think aqua and summery yellow or white and neutral khaki or coral and light blue. The key is to keep the color palette fresh and light.

SIDE TABLES

Painted furniture and shopping the beach are some of the easiest ways to create side tables for your coastal bedroom. Shop yard sales and thrift stores for small pieces of furniture. Paint the pieces in fun, beachy colors to match your décor, lightly distress, and place next to the bed for a simple side table.

diy Why not design your own knobs? Start with a basic wood knob, paint it white, and then glue a shell or piece of coral to the top. You can also create your own drawer pull with rope. Tie a sailor's knot into the rope, thread the rope through the handle holes in the drawer, and secure with another knot.

LAMPS AND SHADES

Table lamps for the coastal bedroom are typically simple and no fuss. For example, the classic design of a white lamp with a white shade works well in any room. Or make your own lamp with a clear glass base kit and shells. Fill the clear glass base with

beach finds, such as shells, starfish, or periwinkles. Then finish the project with a textured shade in linen, khaki, or white.

STORAGE

Place a ladder against the wall to store all the books and magazines that collect at the beach. Add fun hooks just inside the closet to store towels, umbrellas, and beach accessories. Store extra supplies in baskets lined up on a bookshelf with creative labels made from shells. Simply write the contents of the basket on the inside of a shell with a permanent marker, and then tie the shell onto the basket.

TRADITIONAL

Selecting bedding for a traditional space is all about the pattern. Oversized florals, damasks, paisleys, stripes, toile, and Greek key fabrics add drama to the space. Here, the rich patina of a beautiful antique four-poster bed blends well with a neutral duvet cover and patterned fabric.

To re-create this look, start with a set of oversized white pillow shams. Next, layer another pair of shams in a beautiful sienna-and-gold-patterned fabric. Complete the look with a smaller pillow in a light cream and a throw pillow in a traditional gold-and-white stripe.

FARMHOUSE

Farmhouse bedding is all about layers of soft cotton and other organic fabrics. Here, three European shams in hand-dyed gray cotton are layered with white cotton pillow shams. A small throw pillow adds a pop of color.

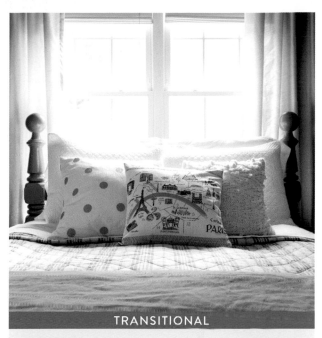

TRANSITIONAL

Beautiful linens and embroidered accents bring a feeling of timelessness to this space. Layers of neutral bedding with down pillows and textured linens accent the simple lines of this room's classic antique furniture.

CONTEMPORARY

This contemporary bedding is all about color, color, and more color. A red, tufted headboard, black-and-white shams, leopard-print pillows, and buffalo check pillows work together to create a dramatic bedding silhouette.

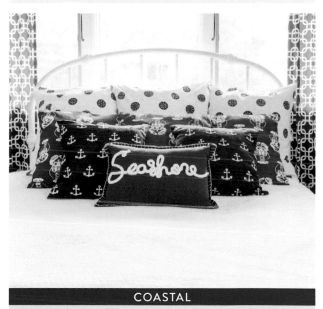

COASTAL

In this coastal bedroom, color and kitschy fabrics work together to add fun and whimsy to the room. Large European shams with navy-and-white sand dollars are mixed with pillows sewn from printed nautical fabrics.

diy

Pom-Pom Throw

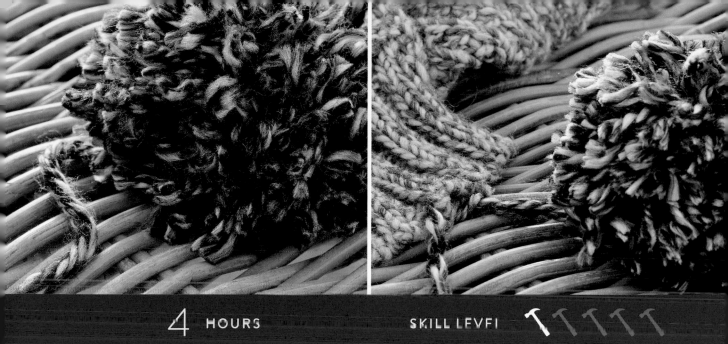

Supplies

a throw with an open weave

chunky yarn

a 4" x 6" rectangular piece of cardboard

scissors

Instructions

1. Start by making the pom-poms. Wrap the yarn around the small piece of cardboard approximately 25 times.

2. Cut another piece of yarn 12" long.

3. Slowly slide the wrapped yarn off the piece of cardboard. Wrap the single 12" piece of yarn around the center and tie tightly. Cut the looped edges and trim and fluff.

4. Repeat steps 1 through 3 until you have 16 pom-poms.

5. Measure the shorter edge of the throw and divide by seven. Using that measurement, start at the corner and tie the pom-poms onto the side of the throw. Continue until you have eight pom-poms tied down one side in equal increments.

6. Repeat step 5 for the opposite side of the throw.

Outdoor Spaces

Sometimes a Porch Just Has to Dance

I grew up in the South, where every porch has a story to tell.

My story?

It's about the day that two tiny princesses put on their crowns.

My twin daughters were born at 29 weeks. They were so tiny—one weighing in at 2.2 pounds and the other at 2.8 pounds. The doctors told us the entire list of potential negative outcomes and bandied about words like *kidney issues* and *brain bleeds* and *vision problems* and on and on and on *until I wanted to scream*.

One afternoon, as the nurse and I sat silently together in the NICU, one of the twins slowly raised her leg into the air and swirled it around. Slowly, she lowered it and raised it and swirled it again. That tiny two-pound girl fighting for her life was trying to dance.

She didn't know the odds. She didn't know about the beeping and monitors and the possible complications and the long journey ahead. She didn't listen to the odds. She didn't worry or fret or care.

She simply danced.

They never looked back, those dancers of mine. God had His hand on them. Each day they grew stronger and bigger and breathed on their own and yawned and stretched and opened their eyes. *And then?* One day they defied all the odds and came home.

Two years later we held their second birthday party on the back porch. It was the finest celebration in the kingdom. There was a princess cake and princess banners and royal party favors and a tiny dance floor decorated with pink polka dots. And in

the center of it all, two tiny princesses spun around in their twirly-whirly skirts and waved their royal scepters and patted their jeweled crowns…

…and danced.

That's the thing about porches. They are places where all the celebrations start. There's something about the easy and the breezy of the sunshine dancing across the floor that creates a warm and welcoming place to curl up on a lazy summer afternoon. Porches are the sweet tea place, the watch a red robin sing place, a lean back against the cushions and count the clouds type of place, the line up the potato salad and baked beans place, and the place to spin and twirl under the stars.

Before we take a look at different types of porches decorated in different styles, let's begin with a few basic principles to take into consideration when designing your porch. If you are refreshing your porch or redecorating your outdoor spaces, here are a few tips to get you started.

Outdoor Materials

This is perhaps the most important thing to take into consideration when you are decorating your outdoor space: Porches are outside. And because they are outside, certain materials extend the life of your porch décor. Luckily, porch décor has come a long way in recent years. So many new materials and surfaces hold up well to outdoor wear and tear.

For example, indoor/outdoor rugs come in a variety of sizes, colors, and materials. Some of the most popular choices include polypropylene, nylon, and polyester. Rugs like these are easy care, resist stains, and can be sprayed off with water to clean.

Textiles

When selecting fabrics for your outdoor spaces, indoor/outdoor fabrics resist stains and mildew from being out in the elements. The good news? These fabrics are bold and vibrant and full of color. The design possibilities are endless when mixing patterns for your space. Make sure to select a variety of patterns, textures, solids, and a few statement textiles for your space to add visual interest.

Plants

One of the easiest ways to introduce color to your space is with plants. Depending on the amount of sunlight your porch receives, choose flowering plants or green, leafy varieties. A fun project for a porch is to create a container garden. When selecting plants for the container garden, you'll want to layer vibrant statement plants with filler plants with trailing vine plants like ivy. The contrast creates a container garden that looks as if it stepped out of the pages of a gardening magazine.

Seating

When choosing outdoor seating for a porch or patio, select pieces made from sturdy materials, such as wicker made from synthetic materials, wrought iron, or teak. Create a seating arrangement from four chairs or two chairs and a love seat. Add a dining table as well for outdoor entertaining. Extra seating on a porch is a must. Add folding chairs for extra guests and cover with cushions or chair covers made from indoor/outdoor fabrics.

Transitional Style Q & A with Laura

Walking through Laura's incredible home, I remember thinking to myself, *Don't blink—you might miss something.* Every detail, every accessory, every furnishing and textile and pillow and rug and chair was so intentional. Design styles were mixed and matched to perfection. It was a home layered with heart and thoughtfulness and deliberate choices. And the best part?

Every piece had a story.

In the middle of the tour, I'd exclaim with delight over this piece or that, and Laura would explain the history—where it came from, what it was, and who its parents were. From the tole trays in the dining room to the wooden shoe mold in the living room to the tiny herb plant on the refrigerator. Every piece had a tale to tell.

That's the intentionality of transitional style.

It's about truly decorating with what you love, no matter the style. It's about a family heirloom sitting next to a planter from Trader Joe's. It's about layering pieces that speak to you and making them work with your existing décor. It's about tossing design rules to the wind and decorating with your heart.

Laura currently lives in the beautiful Hudson Valley of New York State with her husband and two daughters. She and her husband own Finding Home Farms, a maple syrup and home décor brand. The company began as an interior design business that eventually developed into a blog and then evolved into a product-based company. Laura enjoys reading nonfiction books, working on DIY projects around the house, and spending time outdoors. Laura never met a vintage toolbox she didn't want to get into a committed relationship with, and galvanized is her favorite color.

What are your favorite stores to shop at?

My go to for the house are local vintage shops. You never know what you'll find—like the tole trays and the ironstone I used to decorate the hutch in the dining room. For vintage and current artists, I shop Etsy. For example, one of my favorite pieces is from an artist I found on Etsy—The Old Post Road. And my favorite place to shop? My basement. I love to look at things in a new light and repurpose existing pieces.

What one transitional element is a must-have for a space?

One of my must-have elements is any piece made from rustic wood. I include different wood pieces in my spaces, and some of my favorites I use in my home are the ever present toolboxes, the pine dresser in the foyer, and the rustic cutting boards found stacked in the kitchen. We also have a vintage ladder hung between the kitchen and family room that has the Putnam name on a vintage metal tag.

How does your faith influence your design?

My approach to design is simple. I want to create a space where family and friends feel welcome. My goal is always to design warm and welcoming spaces that make you feel immediately at home. Faith is the element and the overriding design principle that ties all of my design choices together.

What's your favorite piece of furniture ever in the history of ever?

My favorite piece of furniture in my home is the bed in the master bedroom. Before I ever bought it, I collected pictures of it from different magazines. I knew the exact style I wanted, and when we finally purchased it, I was so happy. It's a piece with timeless style and classic lines, and it's also made in America.

A Transitional Outdoor Space

Do you have an outdoor space where you want to layer in some transitional style? Here are some specific elements that will introduce a little heart to your home.

FOUND PIECES

Some of Laura's one-of-a-kind pieces come from thrift-store shopping and a little serendipity. She looks for accessories with a story—like a vintage maple syrup bucket with dings and dents and history. Create your own narrative with things that speak to you. Maybe it's the top of a dresser mirror or a set of antique furniture legs or vintage bowling pins with red and blue stripes—each with a tale to tell.

RECLAIMED WOOD

One of the most important elements in a transitional styled space is wood with history. Use reclaimed wood for frames, crates, boxes, or other creative DIY projects. For example, on Laura's mantel is a wood whale she built from wood collected from her grandfather's home.

COLLECTIONS

Decorating with collections is one of the basic elements in a transitional home. Why have one of something when ten is so much better? Popular items to collect include white dishes, candlesticks, wood frames, galvanized watering cans, and vintage books. One of Laura's favorite things to collect is toolboxes. She stacks them up, repurposes them as towel holders, and even creates a Christmas tree for the holidays out of a stack of toolboxes.

REPURPOSED HEIRLOOMS

One fun way to add a little history to a transitionally styled space is with family heirlooms. Repurpose and reuse these pieces of history to lend an air of authenticity to the space. For example, create window treatments out of vintage linens, use silver pieces to organize a countertop, frame an old primer in a shadow box, or mix in architectural fragments to your gallery wall.

TRANSITIONAL STYLE DETAILS

 Create a table from reclaimed wood and vintage table legs.

 Use an oversized crate as a side table.

 Add texture to a space with an oversized rattan light fixture.

4 Wood beams bring character and vintage charm to an outdoor space.

5 Repurpose a galvanized tub as a drink cooler.

6 Add extra seating with an upholstered ottoman.

7 Fill a mason jar with cuttings from the yard.

8 Mix and match textiles for a transitional look.

9 Gather vintage accessories like a galvanized lantern or rattan fishing basket.

Traditional Outdoor Space Style

I never knew how beautiful a field of corn could be until I gazed out at Yvonne's backyard. It was like something out of a movie. You know. The one where the girl used to be a movie star, but she gave it all up to return to her grandmother's farm and start a jelly-making business. When she and her jellies go to the local farmer's market, they run into the quarterback from high school she used to sit behind in geometry class. He takes one look at her, falls in love, and they walk off into the sunset across a cornfield next to an outdoor space with a stone-covered patio and a tree-lined path and gardens full of trellises.

That's an outdoor space—with a little traditional style. Want to add a few winding walkways and rose-covered trellises to your outdoor entertaining area? Here are some style tips to get you started.

ENTERTAINING

Set a traditional style table in your outdoor space with classic linens and white dishes. Layer patterned dishes and silverware atop woven chargers on a wood table. For an easy centerpiece, fill an oversized vase with greenery cut from the yard. Set out vintage salt shakers and sugar containers to bring a little tradition to your table.

diy Create napkin rings from sprigs of boxwood. Place the sprig of boxwood into a glass of water. Let sit overnight until the boxwood forms a ring. Wrap around a napkin and tie off with a small floral wire.

ACCESSORIES

A fun accessory for any porch is an indoor/outdoor rug. When decorating a traditionally styled porch, choose one with a simple graphic design in classic colors such as black and white. Layer indoor/outdoor pillows in a damask, floral, or simple striped pattern. Lastly, lanterns made of wrought iron or reclaimed wood are fun additions.

SEATING

Choose furniture for the back porch that's elegant and functional at the same time. A set of wrought-iron furniture with black cushions and white piping creates a classic look and provides seating in an outdoor space. A metal or wood dining table with matching chairs is perfect for outdoor entertaining. Place a potting bench in the space, and scatter extra seating. You might want to add a worktable to the porch. You know. Just in case you want to start your own jelly business too.

GREENERY

When selecting greenery for the back porch, classic evergreens are some of the best choices. Boxwood, holly, juniper, and yew are all excellent choices for a traditional outdoor space. Choose classic metal urns or wooden planter boxes with clean lines and timeless details.

diy Design your own topiary. Start with a pot of trailing ivy. Shape a wire coat hanger into a circle, twisting the ends together. Place the twisted ends into the pot. Wrap the tendrils of ivy around the wire circle until you've created your own inexpensive topiary.

Farmhouse Style

The year we celebrated graduation outside at the farmhouse in Kentucky was a sight to behold. We pulled out tables and chairs and tossed red-and-white checkered tablecloths on them and added mason jars full of fresh flowers from the yard. We hung banners from the trees and tossed a few outdoor pillows on the ground and ate hamburgers and drank lemonade and sweet tea. There were outdoor games such as badminton and relay races and hula hooping. And the county is still talking about the egg toss.

That's how an outdoor space is used—farmhouse style. Want to add a little farmhouse and some lemonade and hula hooping to your back porch? Here are some style tips to get you started.

ENTERTAINING

When setting the farmhouse table outside, why not make the food the centerpiece? Place a set of wooden pedestals on the table and top with woven baskets of fresh rolls and ironstone platters of fruit and piles of vegetables. Create a clever place setting with terra-cotta pots wrapped with brightly colored bandannas and filled with a bundle of silverware wrapped with jute twine tied with a name tag. Fill mason jars with sweet tea. Layer grapevine wreaths as chargers, and add a tiny wreath of fresh flowers to the back of each chair.

ACCESSORIES

Think fresh and fun when selecting accessories for the farmhouse space. Add giant galvanized metal planters on either side of the screen door, and fill them with trailing vines and flowers. Oversized metal spheres are great accent pieces. Left outside,

they will weather with a beautiful, aged patina. Baskets, white wood planters, and weather vanes all work well on a farmhouse outdoor porch. You can also add drama to the space with billowy curtains made from indoor/outdoor fabric hung from outdoor curtain rods.

SEATING

Hello, porch swing. Nice to meet you. Outdoor porch swings have been hanging around farmhouse porches since sweet tea was invented. Add a set of pillows in a check or stripe in vibrant outdoor fabrics for comfort. Pull up a set of mismatched farmhouse chairs to an outdoor table, and add a wicker love seat and chairs to the space for the perfect conversation spot on a sunny summer afternoon.

GREENERY

Looking for ingredients for your next salad? One fun way to embrace farmhouse style on your outdoor porch is to grow fresh herbs and vegetables in pots. Lettuce, peppers, eggplant, summer squash, and pole beans all grow well in container pots. Place the pots in a sunny place on the porch, and check to make sure your containers have adequate drainage to allow the plants to grow and thrive.

Contemporary Style

Walking out onto Carmel's back porch was like walking into a contemporary art museum. There was color everywhere. From the brilliant green on the walls to the beautiful dark wood planks of the porch to the patterned rug on the floor and the rustic woven blinds and the textured ceiling fan made from reclaimed wood and the bold, black-and-white striped cushions scattered across the furniture, it was a symphony of vivid hues. But to truly celebrate the porch? To understand what color could do for a porch? All I had to do was look up. There on the ceiling was the most incredible sky blue I had ever seen.

That's an outdoor space—contemporary style. Want to add a little contemporary style and a little bit of sky blue to your outdoor porch? Here are some style tips to get you started.

ENTERTAINING

When setting a contemporary style, you want to mix and match different finishes. For example, begin with a bold graphic runner in black-and-white stripes. Add a row of potted succulents in painted terra-cotta pots for the centerpiece. Add black candlesticks and color-blocked place mats in red and orange to complete the look. Lastly, keep outdoor entertaining simple with patterned melamine plates and plasticware in bold, metallic colors such as gold or silver.

ACCESSORIES

Keep things simple when accessorizing an outdoor space. Choose bold pieces that make an impact. For example, a textured throw in a vivid printed pattern makes a statement in an outdoor space. Or select a bold lantern in red or yellow to layer in a pop of color. Make sure to select planters with a sculptural aesthetic to add character and personality.

SEATING

Mix and match furniture to keep the space fresh and ready for entertaining. An oversized table made of steel or a wood tabletop with a live edge are both creative choices for outdoor dining. Select contemporary furniture for the space fitted with bold, graphic cushions in an abstract floral or geometric pattern. For additional seating for a party, folding teak chairs are a great choice.

GREENERY

Plants for an outdoor contemporary space should be colorful with sculptural elements. Flowers such as begonias and impatiens add color to the space. Potted plants such as palm trees, caladiums, and ornamental grasses such as bamboo, purple fountain grass, and New Zealand flax work well on a back porch or other outdoor space. You can also accessorize the back porch with small groupings of succulents in colorful containers.

Coastal Style

Outdoor entertaining in a coastal style setting usually rhymes with lobster. We'd tromp up the winding path from the beach and my mother would have dinner waiting for us on the porch. The table would be set with plates of steaming lobster, ears of corn fresh off the grill, stuffed quahogs, bowls piled high with salad and cut-up vegetables and swordfish so tender it would melt in your mouth. We'd wrinkle our sunburned noses, wiggle our bare feet, wipe the sand away from our seats, and dine like kings.

That's how an outdoor space is used—coastal style. Want to add a little coastal and some wind, waves, and lobster to your back porch? Here are some style tips to get you started.

ENTERTAINING

Celebrate entertaining coastal style with a table set with driftwood and coral. Add a blue-and-white checked tablecloth to your outdoor table, and create a centerpiece with oversized clear vases filled with driftwood and pieces of coral. Lastly, create dramatic flair over the table with a coastal wreath hung from ribbons.

diy Create a coastal place mat. Cut out a rectangular piece of burlap. Fray the edges, and paint a large starfish in the center of the place mat. You could even personalize each place mat and send it home with guests.

ACCESSORIES

With a coastal porch, typically the view is your best accessory. Include vintage lobster crates used as side tables, stuffed poufs made from indoor/outdoor fabric, and knotted rope handles and oversized baskets for beach supplies. Add a row of hooks for towels, umbrellas, and other outdoor accessories. Lastly, display treasures found on the beach, such as shells, starfish, rocks, and sea glass on a shelf.

SEATING

Adirondack chairs are one of the most commonly used seating choices for a coastal back porch. The clean lines and rustic wood lend a nautical feel to the space. Rows of white rockers lined up to face the ocean are the perfect addition to any porch. Fill rockers with pillows made from navy and white fabric, and toss a printed throw over the back for cold coastal nights.

GREENERY

Depending on your coastal setting, there are a wide variety of outdoor plants for your porch. In Florida, choose potted palm trees with their sculptural leaves and height. Elephant ear plants and golden euonymus are also good choices. In

California, select tropical plants like the hibiscus with its brilliantly colored flowers that bloom all summer long. Jasmine and mandevilla also work well in outdoor spaces. And on the shores of the East Coast, plants such as hydrangeas and azaleas are great additions to any summer porch.

Painted Garden Pavers

1 HOUR   **SKILL LEVEL**

Supplies

6" x 6" concrete paver

gray concrete paint

white concrete paint

pencil

stencil

stencil brush

Instructions

1. Paint the concrete paver with white concrete paint. Let dry.

   (Note: This may take two coats.)

2. Place the stencil over the top of the concrete paver. Using the stencil brush, lightly pounce the gray concrete paint onto the paver. Let dry.

3. Repeat steps 1 and 2 for additional pavers.

4. Lay pavers in grass to create a decorative outdoor walkway.

Conclusion

Can you even believe it?

WE DID IT.

We defined our style and took notes and learned about decorating our spaces and discovered what we liked and celebrated our homes and figured out that design comes in different shapes and sizes. But before we leave these pages, I want to mention one more thing. If you take only one idea away from this book. If five years from now you think, *Thistlewood who?* If you mix up your coastal with your farmhouse, and you try to remember what was on page 125, and it all seems a bit fuzzy, I want you to remember this.

You are unique.

And special.

And amazing and wonderful and creative and clever and one of a kind.

Just like your style.

Your style is your own. In this whole world, there is no other style that is EXACTLY like yours. You might be a little bit farmhouse and a little bit contemporary topped off with sprinkles of traditional, and that's perfect. It's perfectly, wonderfully, amazingly YOU. Let your style inspire you instead of define you. I want you to celebrate it and own it and decorate with it and create spaces that make you sing out loud and rooms that make you dance with the sunbeams shining in through your windows.

You got this.

Truly.

Embrace the you that God created you to be...
...and let your style shine.

Resources

Page 34
Paint color: Benjamin Moore Sonnet
Buffet: www.wayfair.com
Rug: www.amazon.com

Page 36
Wall paint color: Benjamin Moore Hazy Skies
Front door paint color: Sherwin-Williams
    Peppercorn

Page 38
Paint color: Sherwin-Williams Portobello

Page 40
Wallcovering: www.lowes.com
Artwork: www.minted.com

Page 42
Paint color: Sherwin-Williams Alabaster
Beach sign: www.christmastreeshops.com

Page 46
Front door paint color: Sherwin-Williams Rachel Pink

Page 59
Pillows: www.walmart.com

Page 60
Paint color: Sherwin-Williams Alabaster
Chairs: www.potterybarn.com
Rug: www.potterybarn
Throw: www.walmart.com

Page 62
Paint color: Benjamin Moore Sonnet
Rug: www.overstock.com
Chairs: www.ethanallen.com

Page 67
Paint color: Benjamin Moore White Heron
Rug: www.target.com
Chair: www.wayfair.com
Sofa: www.wayfair.com

Page 70
Paint color: Benjamin Moore Flowering Herb
Chair: www.ballarddesigns.com
Rug: www.homegoods.com

Page 74
Paint color: Sherwin-Williams
    Shoji White
Table: www.lexmod.com
Lamp: www.target.com

Page 77
Chair: www.westelm.com

Page 92
Wall paint color: Benjamin Moore Sonnet
Ceiling paint color: Benjamin Moore
    Philadelphia Cream

Page 94
Paint color: Glidden Woodsmoke
Wicker chairs: www.wayfair.com
Slipcovered chairs: www.ikea.com

Page 98
Paint color: Sherwin-Williams Argos

Page 102
Paint color: Sherwin-Williams Shoji White
Chairs: www.overstock.com
Table: www.potterybarn.com

Page 104
Beverage cart: www.target.com

Page 106
Paint color: Sherwin-Williams Alabaster
Rug: www.homedepot.com
Pillows: www.walmart.com

Page 124
Paint color: Benjamin Moore Gray Owl
Kitchen Island paint color: Sherwin Williams
   Peppercorn
Bar stools: www.ikea.com

Page 127
Wall paint color: Benjamin Moore Sonnet
Cabinet paint color: Benjamin Moore Atrium White

Page 131
Paint color: Sherwin-Williams Flowering Herbs
Bar stools: www.ballarddesigns.com

Page 135
Paint color: Sherwin-Williams Shoji White
Bar stools: www.wayfair.com
Light fixtures: www.serenaandlily.com

Page 139
Paint color: Sherwin-Williams Alabaster

Page 151
Paint color: Sherwin-Williams Repose Gray

Page 153
Paint color: Sherwin-Williams Peppercorn

Page 155
Paint color: Sherwin-Williams
   Mysterious Mauve

Page 157
Vanity Pain Color: Sherwin-Williams Rachel

Page 159
Paint color: Sherwin-Williams Extra White

Page 174
Paint color: Sherwin-Williams Shoji White
Ceiling paint color: Sherwin-Williams
   Urbane Bronze
Mirror: www.homegoods.com
Pillows: www.homegoods.com

Page 176
Paint color: Benjamin Moore Simply White
Pillows: www.potterybarn.com

Page 180
Paint color: Benjamin Moore Hazy Skies
Bedding: www.craneandcanopy.com

Page 188
Paint color: Sherwin-Williams
   Alabaster
Pillows: www.christmastreeshops.com

Page 206
Outdoor furniture: www.wayfair.com

Page 209
Outdoor furniture: www.hayneedle.com

Page 211
Outdoor furniture: www.jossandmain.com

Page 213
Ceiling paint color: Sherwin-Williams Watery

KariAnne Wood writes the award-winning lifestyle blog *Thistlewood Farms*, a tiny corner of the internet where all the stories and DIY's hang out and drink sweet tea. She also writes, photographs, and styles for several national magazines including *Better Homes and Gardens*, *Romantic Homes*, *Country Women*, and *Flea Market Décor*. KariAnne is the author of *The DIY Home Planner, So Close to Amazing* and *You've Got This (Because God's Got You)*. This fun-loving mother of four, lives in Dallas with her husband. And don't let her red lipstick fool you—her favorite color is actually gray.

Decorate with Confidence

The DIY Home Planner   Available Now

This one-of-a-kind house decorating journal features great tips for every area of home décor, answers to your most commonly asked questions, encouragement and inspiration to get you started, and plenty of space to record your plans and store information. Including convenient pockets, charming illustrations, unique style guides, easy DIY projects, and more!

But Where Do I Put the Couch?   Coming Fall 2019

When you have a decorating dilemma, do you wish you had an expert you could consult? How about two experts?

Popular home decor bloggers Melissa Michaels (*The Inspired Room*) and KariAnne Wood (*Thistlewood Farms*) are teaming up to tackle 101 top decorating questions from people just like you.

Filled with helpful photos and practical solutions, this convenient guide will be your go-to resource for all your home decorating questions.

Connect with KariAnne

www. ThistlewoodFarms.com

@thistlewood

@thistlewoodfarm

@thistlewoodfarm

Join KariAnne in celebrating the incredible, awesome, special individual that is within each of us!